The
Little Windows Book

Kay Yarborough Nelson

Peachpit Press
Berkeley, California

The Little Windows Book

Kay Yarborough Nelson

Peachpit Press, Inc.
1085 Keith Ave.
Berkeley, CA 94708
(415) 527-8555

Copyright © 1991 by Kay Yarborough Nelson

All rights reserved. No part of this book may be reproduced or transmitted in any form or by any means, electronic, mechanical, photocopying, recording, or otherwise, without the prior written permission of the publisher. For information, contact Peachpit Press.

Notice of Liability

The information in this book is distributed on an "As is" basis, without warranty. While every precaution has been taken in the preparation of this book, neither the author nor Peachpit Press, Inc., shall have any liability to any person or entity with respect to any liability, loss, or damage caused or alleged to be caused directly or indirectly by the instructions contained in this book or by the computer software and hardware products described herein.

Trademarks

Throughout this book, trademarked names are used. Rather than put a trademark symbol in every occurrence of a trademarked name, we are using the names only in an editorial fashion and to the benefit of the trademark owner, with no intention of infringement of the trademark. Where those designations appear in this book, the designations have been printed in initial caps.

Library of Congress Cataloging-in-Publication Data

Nelson, Kay Yarborough
 The Little Windows Book / Kay Nelson
    p.   cm.

 ISBN 0-938151-30-4 : $12.95
 1. Microsoft Windows (Computer programs)   I. Title.
 QA76.76W56W45 1990
 005.369–dc2090-48738

0 9 8 7 6 5 4 3 2
Printed and bound in the United States of America

> If you'd have my Advice, I'll give it to you in short,
> for a Word to the Wise is enough,
> and many Words won't
> fill a Bushel.
>
> Benjamin Franklin, introduction to
> *Poor Richard's Almanack*, 1758

Acknowledgments

Many thanks to Matt Kim, for page makeup; Jim Beley, for good advice and tips; Raymond A. Nelson, for patient keystroking and reading; many anonymous reviewers, for their helpful comments; and all the cats, for their continued support.

CONTENTS

1 A Guided Tour 1

What Can You Do with Windows? *1;* Windows and Non-Windows Programs *1;* Get a Mouse! *2;* The Tour Begins *2;* Using a Mouse *3;* Clicking *3;* Double-Clicking *4;* Dragging *4;* Window Basics *5;* The Active Window *5;* Menu Bars *5;* Dialog Boxes *6;* Scroll Bars *6;* Window Icons *6;* The Program Manager *7;* The Groups *8;* The Main Group *8;* Windows and Non-Windows Applications Groups *9;* Games *10*

2 Getting Around in Windows .. 11

Need Help? *11;* Moving in a Window *13;* Keyboard Shortcuts *14;* Selecting from Menus *14;* Using Dialog Boxes *15;* List Boxes *16;* Text Boxes *16;* Check Boxes *16;* Command and Option Buttons *16;* Opening and Closing Windows *17;* Application and Document Windows *17;* Application Windows *18;* Document Windows *18;* Moving between Windows *19;* Arranging Windows and Icons *19;* Moving Windows *19;* Resizing Windows *20;* Maximizing and Minimizing Windows *20;* Arranging Windows *20;* Arranging Icons *23;* Moving Icons *23;* Quick Tips *23*

3 Working with Programs 25

Starting a Program *25;* Starting with the Program Manager *26;* Starting with the Run Command *26;* Starting with the File Manager *27;* Starting with a DOS Command *28;* Using Windows Programs' Menus *29;* Creating, Saving, and Opening Documents *29;* Editing

Documents *31;* The Clipboard *31;* Working with Text *34;*
Moving the Insertion Point *34;* Correcting Mistakes *34 ;*
Selecting Text *35;* Switching between Programs *36;*
Leaving Windows *37;* Quick Tips *37*

4 The Program Manager 39

The Program Manager *39;* Working with the Program
Manager *40;* Group Windows and Icons *41;*
The Window Command *41;* Creating Your Own
Groups *42;* Creating a New Group *42;* Adding a Program
to a Group *43;* Changing the Icon *45;* Adding a
Document to a Group *45;* Adding Programs with
Windows Setup *46;* Changing a Group's Name *48;*
Deleting a Group *48;* Running Programs from the
Program Manager *48;* The Program Manager's
Keyboard Shortcuts *49;* Quick Tips *49*

5 The File Manager 51

Files and Directories *51;* Naming Files *52;* Forbidden
Characters *52;* Popular Extensions *53;* Naming Your
Files *53;* Directories *54;* The Root Directory *54;*
The Path *55;* The File Manager *55;* The Directory Tree *55;*
Seeing the Directory Structure *57;* Expanding and
Collapsing Directories *57;* Looking in a Directory *58;*
File Manager Icons *59;* Climbing the Branches *59;*
Managing Directory Windows *60;* Replace Window
Contents *60;* Cycle Windows *60;* Minimize Windows *60;*
Use the Window Menu *60;* Closing Windows *61;*
Saving Settings *62;* Selecting Files and Directories *62;*
Copying and Moving Files and Directories *63;* Copying *63;*
Wildcards *65;* Moving *65;* Moving Directories *66;*
Renaming Files and Directories *66;* Creating a New
Directory *66;* Deleting Files *67;* Deleting Directories *68;*
Finding Files *68;* Using the View Menu *69;* Sorting a
Display *70;* Listing Files Alphabetically *70;*
Looking at Types of Files *71;* Starting Programs with the

File Manager 71; Dragging a Document Icon 72; Associating Documents and Programs 72; Adding Programs with the File Manager 73; Copying Disks 74; Formatting Disks 75; Other File Manager Secrets 77; Changing the Display 77; Locking a File 77; Printing 77; File Manager's Keyboard Shortcuts 78; Quick Tips 78

6 Customizing Windows 83

The Control Panel 83; Changing Screen Colors 84; Choosing a Color Scheme 84; Your Own Color Scheme 85; Creating Custom Colors 86; Changing Desktop Patterns 87; Choosing a Pattern 87; Changing a Pattern 88; Using Wallpaper 89; Other Desktop Options 90; Icon Spacing 90; Icon Alignment 91; Border Width 91; Cursor Blink 91; Customizing the Keyboard 92; Customizing the Mouse 92; Setting the Date and Time 93; Other Options 93; Customizing Help 94; Quick Tips 95

7 Printing 97

The Print Manager 97; The Print Manager Window 97; Changing the Print Queue 98; Pausing and Resuming Printing 98; Stop That Job! 98; Print Speed 99; Print Manager Messages 99; Network Printing 99; Viewing the Network Queue 100; Printing from Non-Windows Programs 100; Adding Printers 101; Adding a Printer 101; Configuring a Printer 102; The Active Printer 104; Network Printers 104; Fonts 104; Font Basics 104; Adding New Fonts 106; Removing a Font 108; Managing Fonts 109; Changing Fonts 109; Troubleshooting Printing Problems 110; Quick Tips 111

8 Oh, No! (Troubleshooting) ... 113

I'm Out of Memory! *113;* It's Running so S-l-o-w...*113;* Help! I Can't Get Out of My Program! *113;* What Are These Different "Modes"? *114;* It Just Beeps at Me! *114;* I Can't Paste into my Non-Windows Program! *114;* How the *&*% Do I Select Things to Copy to the Clipboard in a Non-Windows Program? *115;* When I Press a Key, Something Else Happens! *116;* I Tiled the Windows, But I Still Can't See Everything! *116;* I Can't Quit Windows! *116;* Help! When I Copy Spreadsheet Data, It's All Jumbled Up! *116;* Uh, oh. What's a Compatibility Warning? *117;* I Can't Run My Pop-Up Programs! *117;* I Can't Run my Non-Windows Program! *117;* What Was That Phone Number Again? *118*

Appendix A *119*

Here's How To...

Appendix B *127*

Keyboard Shortcuts

Index *131*

1

A GUIDED TOUR

If you've never done Windows before, this is the place to start. The short sections in this chapter introduce you to the basics of the **Windows interface**—what you see on the screen, and how you can interact with it.

Windows shields you from the ugly realities of your computer's operating system (DOS) with a graphical user interface that's a lot easier to use than DOS itself. (At least it's easier when you get used to it.) Windows also lets you run several programs at once, each in its own window, as long as you have a computer with enough memory. To switch between programs, you just click with a pointing device called a **mouse**.

What Can You Do with Windows?

Windows also lets you instantly **transfer data** from one program to another, so you can put text typed in your word processing program in your spreadsheet program, and vice versa. This is a feature your friends with Macintoshes have been bragging about for a long time now.

Windows runs all kinds of programs. Sure, it runs programs that were specifically designed for it, such as Microsoft Word for Windows and Excel for Windows, but it will also run other programs, like Lotus 1-2-3 Release 2.2 and WordPerfect 5.1. How this works also depends on what computer you have. If you don't have a 386 computer, programs that weren't designed just for Windows will always appear in full-screen size. If you have a 386 computer, you can run those programs (called "non-Windows applications") in smaller windows, where you can see several programs at once on the screen.

Windows and Non-Windows Programs

CHAPTER 1

Get a Mouse!

A **mouse** is a pointing device that controls the position of the pointer on the screen. It's ideally suited for many tasks and pretty poor at others. What's it good for? It's good for selecting large areas of text, for starting programs by clicking on their icons (those little pictures on the screen), for changing the position of windows on the screen, scrolling through text, and so forth. It's not so good when you're typing to have to take your hands off the keyboard and reach for the mouse.

This means there's a tip in the text.

Yes, you can run Windows without a mouse. But it's tedious. If you don't have a mouse, get one. You won't get the most out of Windows without one. You can get either a bus mouse (one that requires a card inside your computer) or a serial mouse (one that attaches to one of the communication ports on the back of your computer). Either kind comes with instructions for all you need to know to install it. Windows figures out what kind of mouse you have during installation, and it doesn't really matter to it what kind you have. If you haven't got one yet, you'll probably want to ask for a serial mouse, unless you like taking your computer apart and looking at its innards.

Windows has keyboard equivalents for just about everything you can do, but you're really crippled without a mouse. Enough said.

The Tour Begins

If you haven't got Windows started, you may want to start it now so that you can try out some basic techniques during this guided tour. If you've never used a mouse before, it takes some getting used to.

If Windows doesn't come up automatically on your computer, you can start it by typing **win** at the DOS prompt, which will probably be C:\> but may be D:\> or E:\>, depending on your computer.

You'll see the Windows **desktop** when Windows starts. The **Program Manager** is usually the first thing you see. Your screen may look a little different from the one shown here, if you or anybody else has previously used Windows on the computer you're using.

A Guided Tour

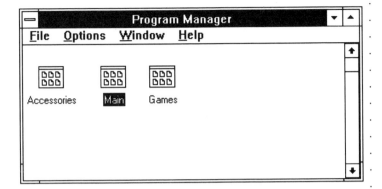

On the desktop, you can organize your work much as you would stack papers and move objects on a real desktop at home or at work. Small pictorial **icons** represent programs, groups of programs, documents, and desk accessories like a calendar or notepad. This desktop is sort of like the Macintosh's famous desktop, but quite a few of its features are different from the Mac's.

The **mouse pointer** is the small solid arrowhead on the screen. As you move the mouse on your real desktop, you'll see the pointer moving on the screen. Try it.

Here's the mouse secret: *you can pick it up.* If you've pushed the mouse all the way to the far corner of your (real) desktop and you're just about to knock over your cup of coffee but what you want is just a little farther over on the screen...pick up the mouse and move it nearer to you. The pointer will stay on the screen where you left it. Try it and see.

You use the mouse in three basic ways: by clicking, double-clicking, and dragging.

To select an item on the screen, you can move the mouse pointer to it and **click** once with the left mouse button. (If you're left-handed, you can change it to the right mouse button, as you'll see in the chapter on customizing Windows.) Selecting an item makes it active, so that you can work with it. For example, you might click on a document's icon so that you could copy or move it.

File Manager

Calendar

Using a Mouse

❗ *You can pick the mouse up! The pointer won't move.*

Clicking

❗ *You have to select something before you can work with it.*

3

CHAPTER 1

Double-Clicking

🛑 *Double-click on an icon to open it*

You can also **double-click** on an item to make it active and actually start it.

To double-click, quickly click twice with the left mouse button. For example, double-clicking on a program's icon will open a window and start the program.

Try opening the Program Manager's Accessories group by double-clicking on its icon.

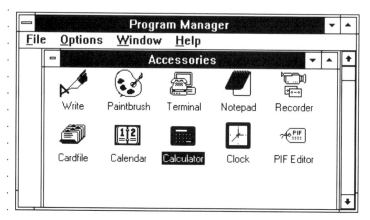

The **Accessories group** contains ten handy utility programs: Windows Write (a simple word processing program), a calendar, a calculator, a painting program, a communications program, and so forth.

Most of these accessory programs are relatively easy and fun to use, so you can explore them on your own when you feel more comfortable with Windows basics.

Dragging

🛑 *To move an icon to another place in the window, drag it.*

A third way of using the mouse is **dragging**. To drag, put the mouse pointer on what you want to drag, press and hold the left mouse button down, and then move the mouse.

Try dragging one of the Accessories program icons and see how easily you can move it to different places inside the window. Release the mouse button when the icon is where you want it.

4

Dragging a window's border is also a way to resize the window and move it around on the screen. If you need to make your Accessories group window larger, try dragging one of its borders outward. You'll see the mouse pointer change shape when it touches the border.

Try opening a window so that you can see what's inside. Double-click on Windows Write, for instance.

Window Basics

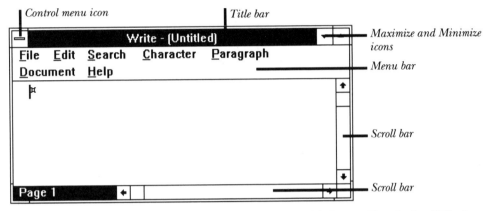

The **title bar** at the top of each window indicates which program is running in the window. Here, "Write - [Untitled]" indicates Windows Write. Untitled just means that you haven't saved any document yet. You can tell which window is active because its title bar is solid.

Only one window can be active at a time.

Just beneath the title bar, you see a **menu bar**. If you click on one of the menu items with the mouse, you'll see a **pull-down menu**. (You can also press Alt and type the letter that's underlined on the menu choice instead of clicking with the mouse.) If you click on File, you'll see the File menu.

Once you've displayed a pull-down menu, you can make additional selections from it by dragging the mouse down to the item you want and then releasing the mouse button. Or you can type the underlined letter.

The Active Window

● *When a window is active, its title bar is solid.*

Menu Bars

Chapter 1

Try choosing About Write... from the Write Help menu. Click on Help, keep the mouse button down, drag the mouse down to About Write..., and release the button.

Dialog Boxes What you see is called a **dialog box**. A dialog box will appear whenever you select a pull-down menu item that has an **ellipsis** (...) next to it. If you choose Open... from the File menu, for example, you'll see a dialog box asking which file to open.

Dialog boxes let you supply additional information that the program needs. This one's asking which group you want to move a program to. (You'll see what that's all about later.) They can also give you information, like the About Write dialog box, or warnings about what you're doing.

Click on OK in the About Write dialog box to close it and get it out of your way.

Scroll Bars Windows often can't display everything that's in a window at once. On the bottom and right sides of a window, you'll sometimes see a **scroll bar**. It indicates that there's more to the document than you can see on the screen. You can click in these scroll bars to move through your documents.

Since there's no document in your Write window, Windows will just beep at you if you try to scroll.

Windows that contain icons can also have scroll bars if there are so many icons that the window's too small to show them all.

Window Icons Icons can also represent small elements of a window. For example, the tiny icons in the upper-right corner of a window (the ones with the up and down arrowheads) are called the **Minimize** and **Maximize** icons. You use these to turn the document or program you're working on into a tiny icon and get it out of your way, or enlarge (maximize) it so that you can work in it again. Try this on the Write window.

Once you've minimized a window, double-click on its icon to enlarge it again.

Another window icon is for a **Control menu**. It's the small box in the upper-left corner of the window, the one that looks like a tiny floppy disk drive. The Control menu will pop up when you click on that icon.

A window's Control menu lets you move and resize windows and switch from one window to another. In most cases, there are easier ways to do what you want than to use them, such as using a keyboard shortcut or the mouse. You'll see lots of these techniques in the next chapter, where we'll look at working with windows in more detail.

To close the Write window so that you can get back to the Program Manager, click on **Close**.

The Program Manager, as you've seen, is the program that automatically starts whenever you start Windows and continues to run in the background while you work. In fact, to exit from Windows, you exit from the Program Manager.

You use the Program Manager to start programs and also to **associate** them into groups so that you can work with them more easily. For example, you might want to create a group of documents relating to one project, such as memo, letters, and budgets, along with your word processing and spreadsheet programs.

The Program Manager, when it first starts (that is, before you or anybody else starts using it), contains just a few **group icons**. A group icon looks like a tiny window with several small icons in it. You'll see how to create your own groups of programs later in the book.

The Program Manager's really in charge of running your programs, so before you go exploring on your own, here's a basic Windows secret, so that you won't get lost. You can always return to the Program Manager to find a program you're running or to exit from Windows.

❢ *Closing a window removes the program from memory. Minimizing a window just makes it into an icon. The program's still in memory.*

The Program Manager

Main

The Main group icon

❢ *Press Ctrl-Esc to get to the Task List and get back to the Program Manager.*

Chapter 1

 It's easy to lose the Program Manager's window, though. Sometimes it can get hidden from view, especially if you have a lot of windows open on your desktop. Here's a trick for finding the Program Manager's window, in case you've lost it. Double-click on the desktop, outside any open windows. This brings up a special window called the **Task List**. See "Program Manager"? Double-click on it to go back to the Program Manager, or double-click on any of the other programs that you're running, to go to them. Click on Program Manager and then on End Task to exit from Windows.

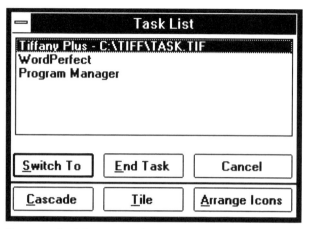

Lost your place? Want to quit? Double-click on the desktop to see the Task List, or press Ctrl-Esc.

The Groups The Program Manager has three groups, until you add more: the Main group, the Accessories group, and (yes!) the Games group. You've seen what's in the Accessories group already, but what about the other two?

The Main Group Double-click on the Main group icon to open it. (If you haven't closed the Accessories group window and it's in your way, click its Minimize icon so that it will politely shrink away.)

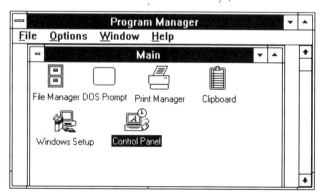

The Main group contains a set of programs that let you set up Windows, print, and manage your filing system, among other things. If your Main group window's not big enough to show them all, click on its **Maximize icon**.

- **File Manager** is a special program that lets you organize your files and directories. Because you can do so much with the File Manager, a whole chapter later in this book is devoted to it.

- **Control Panel** lets you set the colors of your desktop, install printers and fonts, and configure your system.

- **Print Manager** handles local and network printing.

- **The Clipboard** allows you to quickly copy, cut, and paste data among programs.

- **DOS Prompt** takes you out to the familiar C:\> prompt, where you can use the DOS command line.

- **Windows Setup** lets you install Windows programs as well as programs that weren't specifically designed to run under Windows but which will run anyway.

Click on the Minimize icon to shrink the Main group window back to an icon.

When you installed Windows, you could choose whether you wanted Windows to search your hard disk for Windows and Non-Windows applications and create groups for them. If you did this, you'll also see group icons for Windows Applications and Non-Windows Applications in your Program Manager window. (Remember, non-Windows applications are just programs that weren't designed for Windows, like dBASE IV and WordPerfect 5.1.)

You can click on those group icons to see what's in them. If you've purchased Windows programs like Word for Windows or Excel for Windows, you should see their icons when you open the Windows Applications groups.

Windows and Non-Windows Applications Groups

Non-Windows Applications

Chapter 1

Games

Solitaire

Reversi

Games tips

Windows even comes with two games, **Reversi** and **Solitaire**. The object in Reversi is to wind up with more red circles than blue ones on the screen when you're done (white circles if you don't have a color monitor). In Solitaire, you're trying to build the four suits in order, just like in the card game. When you win, you get a great animated screen display. The Game menu in both programs lets you specify how some of their features work.

- In Solitaire, double-click on aces to start your stacks; then double-click on cards to build the stacks.
- In Reversi, press Tab to see what the possible moves are.

That's the fifty-cent tour of Windows basics, enough to get you started playing Reversi, at least. If you want to explore on your own, you can get more help by choosing Help from a window's menu bar. In the next chapter, you'll see more about working with Windows, including more about getting help.

2

WORKING WITH WINDOWS

Windows has what's called a "rich interface." That's a fancy way of saying there are several zillion ways to do just about anything, either by using the mouse or by using the keyboard. This chapter tries to sort out some of the easiest ways to get basic tasks done, so that you can quickly get started using Windows. Later, when you're more comfortable with the program, you can explore other methods on your own. Like the stork theory, it won't quite cover all the details, but it'll do for now.

Just about the most basic skill you need in Windows is how to get help when you need it. To be able to get help efficiently, you'll need to know how to use menus, move around in a window, and use dialog boxes, so we'll look at those things first, in a little more detail than the quick tour in Chapter 1. Then we'll look at all sorts of ways you can arrange windows on your desktop.

You can get help on what you're doing in Windows by clicking on **Help** in the window's menu bar (pressing Alt-H will do it, too) or just by pressing the function key F1. Pressing F1 is the same as choosing Index from the Help menu. It gets you the help index, where you can find help on any Windows program, and Windows itself.

Need Help?

Pressing F1 gets you the Windows help index.

In fact, you can get help on using Help by just choosing Help from the Help menu! On the next page is the beginning of this Help window.

Once you've displayed the help system, you can get help in several different ways, Help has icons called Index, Back, Browse (forward and back), and Search that let you

Chapter 2

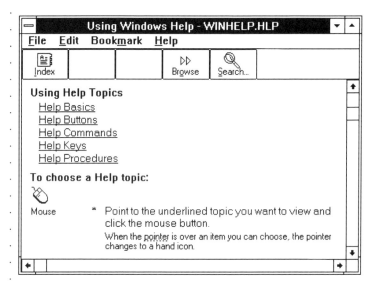

jump around between topics. Clicking on one of the **Browse** icons will show the previous topic in the help system, or the next one. If the Browse icon is gray, there isn't any previous or next topic.

If you click on the **Search** icon, you'll see a list of key words and phrases. Highlight the one you want and then choose Search. You'll see a list of topics. Highlight one and click on Go To to get a help screen on that topic.

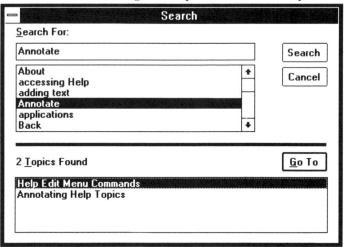

Working with Windows

Another way to get help is to click on one of the words or phrases that are underlined, such as "Help Basics" in the first help screen. You'll immediately go to that topic. If you click on one of the words or phrases with a broken underline (like "pointer" in the figure), you'll get a pop-up window showing its definition. Keep the mouse button pressed down to read it; when you release the button, the window goes away.

You can also use the Help menu bar at the top of the screen, just as in any Windows program. (More on selecting from menus shortly.)

If there's more to the help screen than can fit in one window, you can **scroll** to see the rest of it.

Windows often can't display everything that's in a window at once. (This is almost always true of help windows.) On the bottom and right sides of a window that contains more than what's showing, you'll see a **scroll bar**. It indicates that there is more in the window than you can see on the screen. You can use these scroll bars to move through a document or text that's displayed in a window.

Moving in a Window

To move downward toward the end of the text, you can click in the lower part of the vertical scroll bar, or you can click on the small empty box in the scroll bar and drag it down. To move backward to the beginning of the text, click in the upper part of the scroll bar, or drag the empty box up. You can also move the mouse pointer to the boxes containing the up and down arrows, and press and hold the left mouse button down to scroll up or down.

 Quick scrolling

A quick way to move through a long document is to click in the scroll bar at just about the place where you want to go. To go to the end of the document, click at the end of the scroll bar. Click in the middle to go to the middle. You get the idea.

You can scroll horizontally by using the scroll bar and scroll boxes at the bottom of the window.

Chapter 2

Sometimes the keyboard's faster for scrolling than reaching for the mouse. On the keyboard, use the PgUp and PgDn keys. Press Ctrl-Home or Ctrl-End to go to the beginning or end of what's in the window.

Keyboard Shortcuts

Up to now, most of your practice has been with the mouse, but, as you just saw, you can also type at the keyboard. You may find that it's easier to use the mouse for making selections at first. Later, after you're used to Windows, you'll use the keyboard more.

Sometimes it's faster to use the mouse—to start a program by double-clicking on its icon, for example. But sometimes using keyboard shortcuts is faster, especially if you're typing along.

If a menu choice has a keyboard shortcut, you'll see it listed next to the item on the menu. On this Windows Write menu, notice that everything has a keyboard shortcut!

Windows has many keyboard shortcuts that you can use to speed up your work. After you work with Windows for a while, you'll probably memorize most of the shortcuts for what you do most often. A lot of them aren't on the menus, but you'll see what those are as we go along.

 A big chart at the back of the book lists all the shortcuts and techniques, so if you need to look one up, you'll find them all in one place.

Selecting from Menus

Working with one Windows program is very similar to working with another, because you use the same basic methods for issuing commands, cutting and pasting, and switching from one program to another.

The menus you see on the menu bars depend on which program is running in the window. You'll get a File menu and an Edit menu in all Windows programs, but the rest of the menus may be different. If you're running Microsoft Excel, for example, the choices will be File, Edit, Gallery, Chart, Format, and so forth. In Microsoft Word they'll be File, Edit, View, Insert, and so on.

Working with Windows

Remember from Chapter 1 that when you click on a menu choice in the menu bar (or press Alt and type the underlined letter), you'll get a **pull-down menu**.

You can select a choice from a pull-down menu by

- Clicking on it
- Typing the letter that's underlined (either lowercase or uppercase will do)
- Typing the shortcut key listed to the right of the option.

Sometimes combining keyboard shortcuts can save you several mouse operations. For example, pressing Alt-F and then typing O is a shortcut for selecting File from the menu bar and then choosing Open.

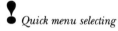 *Quick menu selecting*

If a menu choice is gray, you can't select it. If there's a check mark next to it, it means that the choice is always either on or off, and it's on. (Selecting it again will turn it off.) If there's an arrowhead next to an item, selecting it will bring up another menu. If there's an ellipsis (...), selecting that choice will bring up a dialog box.

Dialog boxes come up to ask for some other information that the program needs, or to verify that you really want to carry out a command. When you see a dialog box, you'll need to fill it out with the correct information (how you do this depends on what kind of a box it is) and then press Enter or click OK.

Using Dialog Boxes

To move around in a dialog box, press Tab (Shift-Tab moves you backward) or just point and click with the mouse.

To back out of a dialog box without changing anything, just click Cancel, press Esc, or double-click in the Control icon to close the box. Windows will beep at you if you click outside the box to leave it. Very annoying.

Quick selecting: Type the underlined letter to go straight to a selection in a dialog box.

15

CHAPTER 2

List Boxes — You can scroll through **list boxes** with their scroll bars. When you see what you want, click on it to highlight it. If you don't have a mouse, you'll have to press Alt plus the underlined letter of what you want to choose, and you'll have to scroll with the PgDn and PgUp keys or the arrow keys.

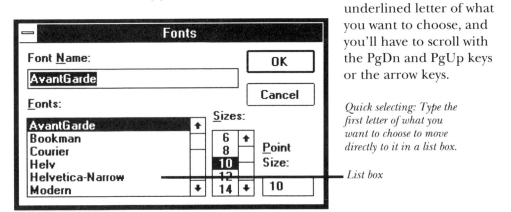

Quick selecting: Type the first letter of what you want to choose to move directly to it in a list box.

— *List box*

Text boxes — If the dialog box is a **text box**, you'll need to type information the program needs. Here it's asking what you want to find. First, click in the text box; then type the information. The insertion point is indicated by an **I-beam**. You can use the regular editing keys, like Backspace, to correct any errors you make as you type. You can also select text by dragging over it.

Text box
Check box

Check Boxes — You use **check boxes** to turn a feature off (not checked) or on (checked). Click with the mouse to check or uncheck something. Without a mouse, the space bar toggles the check mark on and off.

Command and Option Buttons — **Option buttons** are round. Only one option button in a group can be selected. Click on the one you want to choose it. To deselect an option, click on another one.

Without a mouse, press Tab to get to the button you want. A dashed line will surround it when you can choose it. Then press the space bar to select it.

Command buttons, like OK and Cancel, are square. If a command button has a bold outline around it, you can just press Enter to select it.

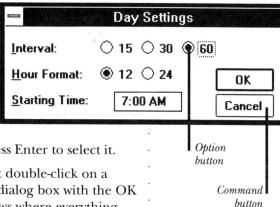

Option button

Command button

In some dialog boxes, you can just double-click on a button to choose it and close the dialog box with the OK button. This is one area in Windows where everything doesn't always work the same way, though. Try double-clicking to see if this will work in your dialog box.

You'll be opening and closing windows a lot. The quickest way to open one is to double-click on its icon.

To close a window, you have several options. If you've got the mouse in your hand, the fastest way is just to double-click on the window's Control menu icon. If your hands are on the keyboard, pressing **Alt-F4** is probably faster. (If that doesn't work, try **Ctrl-F4**.) You can also choose Close from the window's Control menu.

If you try to close the Program Manager's window, you'll get a dialog box asking if you want to leave Windows. Click cancel if you don't want to, or OK if you do. It's very easy to do this when what you really want to do is close the Accessories group window or the Main group window, for instance. This happens because there are really two different kinds of windows in Windows.

There are basically two kinds of windows in Windows: **application windows**, which contain programs, like the Program Manager or the File Manager or Windows Write, and **document windows**, which are windows that belong to a program. *They don't necessarily hold documents!*

Document windows can also hold groups of programs, like the Program Manager's Accessories and Main groups.

Opening and Closing Windows

❗ *Closing a window removes the program from memory.*

❗ *Double-clicking on a group window's Control icon turns the window into an icon.*

Application and Document Windows

Chapter 2

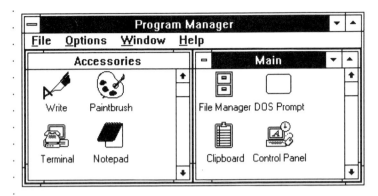

Most of the time, you never have to worry about which is which: you can just click in either kind of window to make it active. (The keyboard shortcuts are sometimes different for the different types of windows.)

🛑 *Application windows have menu bars.*

There's an easy way to tell the difference between an application window and a document window: an application window has a menu bar.

Application Windows

If the program that you're running can handle only one document at a time, the document will be in the application window. You'll see the name of the program on the title bar with the name of the document, if it's been saved. For example, you might see "Notepad - TEST.TXT". That would indicate you're running Notepad (a program that comes with Windows) and working on a document named TEST.TXT. If you haven't saved the document yet, the title bar will say "[untitled]".

🛑 *The Program Manager and Help are application windows.*

Document Windows

If the program that you're running can work with more than one document at the same time, you can have separate document windows associated with that program. For example, the Windows File Manager lets you open several directories at once, each in its own window. Microsoft Word and Excel for Windows also let you have several documents open at once.

Document windows all use the parent application window's menu bar. If you open the Accessories or Main groups, you'll see that the menu is on the Program Manager window.

The Windows manual lists all sorts of different ways you can manipulate application windows and document windows. Figuring out which is which can be confusing when you're new to Windows. Using Alt-F4 vs. Ctrl-F4 to close the window is one of the confusing things. Alt-F4 closes a document window, and Ctrl-F4 closes an application window. Until you get used to the difference (if ever), just double-click on a window's Control menu icon (in the upper-left corner) to close the window, or click on its Minimize icon (in the upper-right corner) to make it into an icon.

> *Just click in a window, no matter what kind it is, to make it active.*

In addition to clicking in the window you want to go to, there are other ways to move from window to window:

Moving between Windows

- You can display the **Task List** (with Ctrl-Esc or by double-clicking on the desktop), highlight the name of the program you want to switch to, and choose Switch To (or just double-click on the program's name).

- You can press **Alt-Esc** to cycle through application windows (those that have title bars).

> *Pressing Alt-Esc is the fastest way to cycle through all the programs you've got running.*

- You can press **Ctrl-Tab** (or choose Next from the Control menu) to cycle through document windows (those without title bars.) This is a convenient way to switch between different windows in the Program Manager, such as Main, Games, Accessories, and so forth.

As you work with Windows, your screen can get cluttered very quickly. Here are a few basic techniques you can use to arrange the windows on your desktop so that you can see what's in them.

Arranging Windows and Icons

Moving Windows

The easiest way to move a window is to drag it by its title bar. Click with the mouse in the title bar and, still holding the mouse button down, drag the window to where you want it.

Chapter 2

> You can move a dialog box, too, if it has a title bar: just drag it by the title bar. This is handy if a big dialog box is in the way of something you need to read on the screen.

The **Control menu** (the one under the little icon in the upper-left corner of the window) also has a Move command. You can choose Move and then press the arrow keys on the keyboard to move the window, pressing Enter when you've got it where you want it, but it's faster just to drag the window by its title bar.

Resizing Windows

You may also want to make a window smaller or larger. Here again, this is a job for the mouse.

Move the mouse to one of the borders of the window. You'll see the pointer change shape to a two-headed arrow. When it changes shape, press the mouse button down and drag the window in the direction you want to go—outward to enlarge it, or inward to make it smaller. For example, to shrink it down to a smaller box in both directions, put the mouse pointer on one of the window's corners (it will change to the double arrowhead here, too) and drag it inward.

> *Quick sizing: drag the lower-left corner inward.*

Yes, you can use the Control menu's Size command here too, (press the right arrow or left arrow keys until you've resized the window; then press Enter) but why bother? You move only one step at a time.

Maximizing and Minimizing Windows

The **Maximize** and **Minimize** icons in the upper-right corner of a window will shrink the window down to an icon or enlarge it to full-screen size. Minimizing a window when you're temporarily through working with it is a good idea because it keeps the screen from becoming too cluttered. You can just double-click on its icon to open it again.

> Minimizing a help window with a lot of information in it that you're referring to back and forth is a good way to keep it handy.

> Keep in mind that minimizing a window isn't the same as closing it! When you close a window, the program is

removed from memory. When you minimize a window, it's still in memory, ready to use, just out of your way.

What if you maximize a window to full-screen size and then want to make it smaller? You can try and try to make the mouse pointer change to a double-headed arrow by moving it to a corner of the window, but it won't work! The trick here is to click on the **Restore icon**. It replaces the Maximize icon in the upper-right of the window when the window's full screen size. Clicking there restores the window to the size it was before you made it full-screen size. Subtle, huh? I had a hard time finding it.

Click on this icon to restore a window to its former size

If you don't want to arrange Windows by hand (or by mouse), you can use the program's built-in Tile and Cascade commands. They're on the Window menu and also on the Task List. If you choose Tile, the open windows will become smaller to fit across your desktop:

Arranging Windows

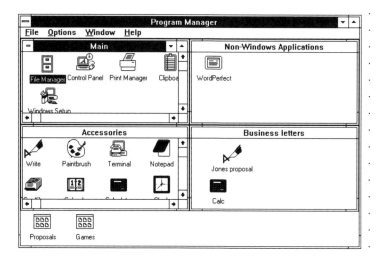

Choosing **Cascade** arranges the windows so that only their title bars are showing:

Chapter 2

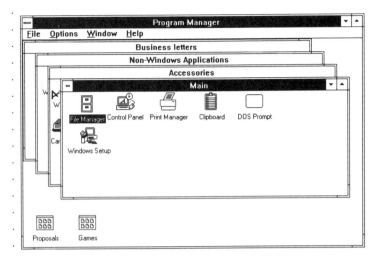

● *Tiling vs. cascading?* You'll find that tiling windows is useful if you're copying or cutting and pasting material between several different programs, because you can see more of what you're cutting or copying and where it's to go. Cascading is useful if you're working in only one window at a time but have several windows open and want to be able to see their title bars, so that you can remember what they are.

The keyboard shortcuts are Shift-F4 for Tile and Shift-F5 for Cascade.

● *Find hidden windows by tiling (Shift-F4) or cascading (Shift-F5).* Even after you tile (or cascade) all your document windows, you may find that some windows are still hidden on your desktop. Here's the trick for cascading or tiling everything on the desktop: First, arrange all the application windows by bringing up the Task List (double-click on the desktop or press Ctrl-Esc) and choosing Cascade or Tile. Then choose Cascade or Tile from each application's Window menu (if it has one) to arrange all the document windows. (If you're running a non-Windows program, it won't have a Window menu.)

● *Save your windows arrangement!* Here's a hint: Once you've arranged windows as you'd like them, be sure to click **Save Changes** when you exit Windows. That way, the next time you start Windows, your windows will be arranged the same way you left them.

Windows also has some built-in commands for arranging icons. You already saw how the Minimize box will shrink a window down to an icon. Well, the Task List and the Program Manager's Window menu both have an **Arrange Icons** command that will line up icons neatly. If your screen gets very cluttered, try it. (You'll see how to change the spacing between the icons in the chapter on customizing Windows.)

Arranging Icons

The Arrange Icons command only works in the window that's active. To arrange all your icons, choose Arrange Icons, close all your group windows, and then open them again.

Moving an icon in a window is easy. Just drag it to where you want it. You can even drag it into another group window. Press Ctrl when you drag if you want to make a copy of it.

Moving Icons

Drag an icon to move it, or press Ctrl and drag it to copy it.

You won't be allowed to drag an icon out of one of the Program Manager's groups and onto the desktop. To get an icon out on the desktop where it'll be handy for you to use, open it (double-click on it) and then minimize it.

Moving icons to the desktop

Here's a quick rundown of the techniques you learned in this chapter, plus some of the (often obscure) keyboard shortcuts.

Quick Tips

Here's How To...

Get help	Click on Help on the menu bar, press Alt-H, or, to get the help index, press F1.
Move in a window	Drag or click in the scroll bars, or click on the arrow icons.
Select from menus	Click on the item or press Alt and type the underlined letter or number. When the pull-down menu appears, click on the item, or type the underlined letter or

Here's How To...*(continued)*

	number. You can also highlight the name with the arrow keys and press Enter.
Move within a dialog box	Click in it, or press Tab to move forward or Shift-Tab to move backward.
Choose an item in a dialog box	Click on the selection, or type Alt-*letter* (where *letter* is the letter in the box).
Scroll a list dialog box	Click on the up or down arrow in the scroll box, or type Alt-*letter* and then press the down arrow key.
Open a window	Double-click on its icon or press Enter when the icon is highlighted.
Close a window	Double-click on its Control icon (or press Alt-F4 in application windows; Ctrl-F4 in document windows).
Switch to a different window	Click in it, double-click on its name in the Task List, or press Ctrl-Tab for document windows; Alt-Esc for application windows.
Move a window	Drag it by its title bar or use the Control menu's Move command.
Size a window	Drag it outward or inward by its corner, or use the Control menu's Size command.
Maximize a window	Click on its Maximize icon or choose Maximize from its Control menu.
Minimize a window	Click on its Minimize icon or choose Minimize from its Control menu.
Restore a window	Click on its Restore icon or choose Restore from its Control menu.
Tile windows	Choose Tile from the Windows menu or press Shift-F4.
Cascade windows	Choose Cascade from the Windows menu or press Shift-F5.

3

WORKING WITH PROGRAMS

All Windows programs have a few things in common, in addition to how you work with their windows. You start them all the same way, and once you're in them, you'll find similar menus in them. This chapter takes a look at some of the techniques Windows programs (and even non-Windows programs—those that aren't designed especially for Windows) have in common.

If you're like me, you want to get started working with programs *right away,* before you wade through a lot of details that you may never use about the Program Manager and File Manager. In fact, if you're really lucky and all the programs you'll be using are already in Program Manager groups, you may not need to use the Program Manager to create new groups until later, and you may not need to use the File Manager until quite a bit later, if at all.

The techniques in this chapter can get you started using the basics of Windows programs. If you see something you need more information about (like working with directories, for example) you can go to one of the other chapters to find out more about it.

If the program you're starting is a Windows program, it will appear in a window. If it's not a Windows program, you'll probably first see it in a **full screen** when it starts.

If you have a 386 computer, you can press Alt-Enter to make a non-Windows program run in a smaller window. Pressing Alt-Enter again will return it to full-screen size.

Starting a Program

Chapter 3

You have several choices of ways to start a program running under Windows. Here are a few of them.

- If the program's part of a group, it's easiest to start the program in the **Program Manager** by double-clicking on the program's icon.

- If the program's not part of a group, you can use the **Run command** in either the Program Manager or the File Manager (it's on the File menu in both).

- You can go out to DOS by clicking on the **DOS Prompt** icon (in the Main group) and start the program running in DOS.

There are a couple of other ways you can start programs from the File Manager, but since they're a little tricky, we'll save them for that chapter.

Starting with the Program Manager

The easiest way to start a program is to double-click on its icon in the Program Manager. First, double-click on the group icon that contains the program you want to start; then double-click on the icon of the program you want to use.

 Pressing Ctrl-Esc will bring up the Task List, if you've lost the Program Manager!

If you've been working with Windows, you may have minimized the Program Manager's icon, or there may be so many windows open on your desktop that you can't find it. Double-click on the desktop (outside any windows or icons); then double-click on Program Manager in the Task List.

If you use a program often, you'll probably want to put it in a group so that you can start it by clicking on its icon in the Program Manager. You'll see how in the next chapter.

Starting with the Run Command

Programs that you hardly ever use can take up unwanted space in your Program Manager window. Instead of adding a little-used program to a group, you can start it by using the Program Manager's Run command.

```
┌─────────────── Run ───────────────┐
│ Command Line: [              ]    │
│           ☐ Run Minimized         │
│        [  OK  ]  [ Cancel ]       │
└───────────────────────────────────┘
```

From the File menu, choose Run. Then enter the command you usually use to start the program from DOS and click OK (or just press Enter). For example, to start WordStar, enter *ws*. To specify a document to work with, enter its name after the program's command. For example, entering *ws budget.wsd* would start WordStar and open a WordStar document named BUDGET.WSD.

This works fine as long as the program is stored in the Windows directory, or if you've previously told DOS where it's stored by using the DOS PATH command. If not, you have to enter the program's path instead of just the command you use to start it. As far as Windows is concerned, *path* means "all of the directories that lead to the directory where the program is stored plus the command you use to run the program."

If this doesn't make sense to you yet, use one of the other ways to start the program until you read the File Manager chapter, where the mysteries of paths and directories and other DOS tricks will be explained.

If you don't want to work with the program immediately but would like it to be handy on your desktop, easy to find when you're ready to use it, click **Run Minimized** in the Run box. That will shrink it down to an icon and you can open it whenever you like by double-clicking on it. How tidy.

Click Run Minimized to keep your desktop neat.

If you don't use the Run command, you can just click on the minimize icon to turn the program into an icon until you're ready to use it.

You can also start a program by using the File Manager. (You'll see a lot more about the File Manager in Chapter 5.) Just double-click on the File Manager's icon, double-click on the directory the program is in (directories look like tiny folder icons) and then double-click on the program's name when the list of what's in the directory comes up.

Starting with the File Manager

File Manager

CHAPTER 3

How can you tell what's a program? Programs always have a .EXE or a .COM extension. Their icons look different from document icons or directory icons, too. Look closely; you'll see.

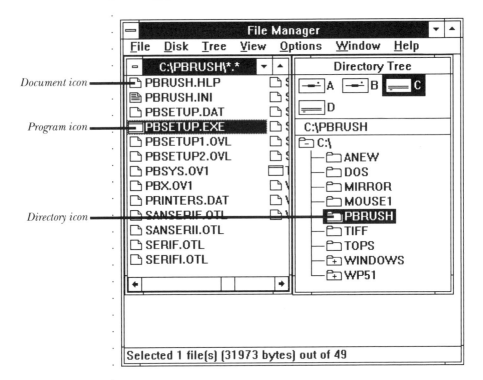

Document icon
Program icon
Directory icon

You can also use the File Manager's File menu, choose the Run command, and then enter the command used to start the program you want to run, just like using the Program Manager's Run command.

Starting with a DOS Command

Well, if you really want to use DOS... you can click on the **DOS Prompt** icon (it's in the Program Manager's Main group). That takes you out to the C:\> prompt, where you can start programs from the command line and work with them in DOS, without even knowing that Windows is there. When you're finished working in DOS, return to Windows by typing *exit* and pressing Enter.

DOS Prompt

❗ *To get back to Windows from DOS, type **exit** at the DOS prompt.*

28

Working with Programs

Any Windows program you run will undoubtedly have **File**, **Edit**, and **Help** menus. This is part of Windows' "standard interface," so that once you understand how to do a common task, you don't have to learn it all over again in another program.

Using Windows Programs' Menus

You use the File menu for creating new files, saving them, and opening files you've already created. This one's for the File menu for Windows Write, but there are New, Open, Save, and Save As commands on all File menus.

Creating, Saving, and Opening Documents

Choose **New** whenever you want to start a brand-new, empty document. If a document's already on your screen, you'll get a chance to save it before Windows clears the screen to start the new document.

```
New
Open...
Save
Save As...
Print...
Printer Setup...
Repaginate...
Exit
```

Choose **Open** when you want to open a document that's already been saved. You'll see a dialog box where you can click on the document you want to open. Use the scroll bars if the name of the document you want isn't displayed on the screen.

```
                    File Open
Filename:  *.TXT                          OK
Directory: c:\windows                     Cancel
Files:              Directories:
3270.txt            [..]
networks.txt        [system]
printers.txt        [-a-]
readme.txt          [-b-]
sysini.txt          [-c-]
sysini2.txt         [-d-]
sysini3.txt
winini.txt
winini2.txt
```

Windows will automatically display the contents of the current directory (this will usually be the Windows directory) and will automatically show you the files that normally belong to the program you're using. For

> *To see all the files in the directory, enter *.* in the Filename: box.*

example, if you're in Windows Write, you'll see all the files with a .WRI extension. If you're running the Notepad, you'll see all the files with a .TXT extension. The File Manager chapter has a chart that shows what all these extensions are and which programs they belong to, if you're interested.

> To go directly to a document name in a long list, click in the box the list is in and then type the first letter of the name.

If you look through the whole list and don't see the document you're looking for, it isn't in the current directory. To see the list for another directory, click on [..] under "Directories:". This will take you up one level of directories. If you're not sure what directory the document you want is in, you can use the File Manager to find it, as you'll see later in the book. If you're not sure what a directory is in the first place... see the File Manager chapter.

Choose **Save** when you're ready to save your work. If you haven't saved the document before, you'll get the **Save As** dialog box, where you can enter a name and specify the directory where you want to store the saved file.

If you want to save the document you've been working on under another name, use the Save As command instead of Save.

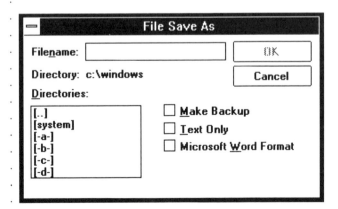

A few commands will also be common to all Edit menus, no matter what program you're using. For example, Windows provides an **Undo** command that miraculously undoes whatever you did last. (Alt-Backspace is the keyboard shortcut for it.) You can restore text you deleted by mistake, change formats back to what they were before, and so forth. If what you did can't be undone, the Undo choice will be gray.

Editing Documents

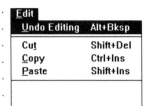

Keep in mind that Windows only remembers *the last thing you did*, and that's all it can undo.

You'll also see **Cut**, **Copy**, and **Paste** commands on the Edit menu. As their names imply, you use them just as you would use scissors and glue to cut and paste material you've selected in the program you're working with. What's new about them in Windows is that when you cut or copy something, it also goes to a special area called the **Clipboard**, where it can be pasted into a completely different program from the one you're using.

The Clipboard

Clipboard

When you cut text (or graphics), it doesn't really go away. Instead, it goes to the Clipboard. You can paste it into another place in your document, or into any other document, for that matter. You can even paste it into documents of other programs.

When you copy text, the copy goes to the Clipboard, too, so you can paste what you copy as well as what you cut. You can even copy between non-Windows programs.

To cut something, select it (usually by dragging over it to highlight it); then choose Cut from the Edit menu (or press Shift-Del). It will disappear from your document. At this point, it's on the Clipboard.

To copy something, use the same process: select it and then choose Copy (or press Ctrl-Ins). It stays in your document and a copy goes to the Clipboard.

To paste what you've cut or copied, put the insertion point where you want it to appear (just clicking with the mouse is easiest, but you can use the arrow keys, too). Remember, this can be somewhere else in the document (this is how you move text) or somewhere else in another document, or somewhere else in another program. Then choose Paste or press Shift-Ins. The contents of the Clipboard will appear.

Because you use these operations frequently as you edit documents, you'll probably want to get used to the keyboard shortcuts for them so that you don't have to take your hands off the keyboard. Here they are, all together:

Ctrl-Ins   **Copies** whatever you've selected

Shift-Del **Cuts** whatever you've selected

Shift-Ins **Pastes** whatever you've cut or copied

One way to remember these last two easily is that you're *shifting* something from one place to another when you cut and paste.

To cut or copy more than what's showing in a window, keep the right mouse button down and scroll to select it, or click at the beginning of the selection, press the Shift key, and click at the end of the selection. Pressing the Print Screen (or PrtSc) key will copy the contents of the screen.

To cut or copy graphics in a painting program like Windows Paintbrush, use the scissors or lasso tools. In a drawing program, such as PageMaker or Corel DRAW!, click or Shift-click to select objects. Some programs, like Excel, let you select by using menus.

You can use the Clipboard in non-Windows programs, too.

If you're in a non-Windows program, the Paste and Copy commands (no Cut; sorry) will be on the Edit menu that you access from the **Control menu**. (Double-click on the Control icon in the upper-left corner of the window, or press Alt-Space bar; then choose Edit.)

You need to be running the program in a window (not full screen) to do this. To see if your non-Windows program will run in a window, press Alt-Enter while you're running it full screen. If it won't, there's still a way to copy. See the "Oh, No! (Troubleshooting)" chapter.

Once you click with the mouse in a non-Windows program running in a window, Windows thinks you're trying to select something so that you can put it on the Clipboard. If you look at the menu bar at the top of the screen, you'll see "Select..." and the name of the program. If you try to do *anything*, Windows will beep at you. If you try to go back to a full screen, it will show you a dialog box complaining that it "cannot switch to full-screen mode." *Press Esc or the right mouse button* to get out of this situation.

❗ *Stuck in a non-Windows program?*

See the "Oh, No!" chapter for more of these handy tips about working with non-Windows programs.

You can cut, copy, and paste text, data from a spreadsheet, graphics (although graphics won't always work if you're in a non-Windows program) results you've calculated with the Calculator, notes you've jotted in the Notepad—just about anything.

Once something's in the Clipboard, you can paste it over and over again; it doesn't go away until you cut or copy again.

Get used to the Clipboard; it can change the way you've been working up till now.

❗ *Let the Clipboard do the walking!*

For example, you can use the Clipboard to save yourself a lot of typing time when a program asks you for information in dialog boxes. Suppose you want to find a certain phrase in Windows Write. Highlight the phrase and press Ctrl-Ins for Copy; then paste it in the Find dialog box instead of typing it again and maybe making a mistake.

To see what's in the Clipboard, double-click on its icon (it's in the Program Manager's Main group). What you copied or cut may not look just exactly as it did in the program, but don't worry: it'll be fine when you use it in another program.

Be careful: the next time you cut or copy, the data that was in the Clipboard will disappear, and the newly cut or copied data will take its place. Make sure you've pasted

Chapter 3

before you cut or copy again. If there's something in the Clipboard that you want to keep, you can save it as its own file by choosing Save As from the Clipboard's File menu (leave the .CLP extension if you want to use it again in the Clipboard). Once you've saved it, you can bring it back into the Clipboard by using the Open command.

 Deleting and cutting aren't the same thing!

Also, keep in mind that **deleting** and **cutting** aren't the same thing, not by a long shot. When you delete (with the Del or backspace keys), that material doesn't go to the Clipboard, and you can't get it back by pasting. Use the Undo command to get material you've deleted by mistake. Use the Paste command to paste what you just cut.

Working with Text

All Windows programs use the same techniques for basic text entry and editing. Here's a brief rundown.

Moving the Insertion Point

The trick to moving the **insertion point** (the I-beam pointer in a document or text box) is to remember that you have to have a place in the document to move it to. If you haven't created any blank lines by pressing Enter or the space bar in a new document, there's nowhere to go.

To go to	Press
The next or previous line	Down arrow or Up arrow
The next or previous word	Ctrl-Right arrow or Ctrl-Left arrow
The end or beginning of a line	End or Home
The end or beginning of the document	Ctrl-End or Ctrl-Home
The next or previous screen	PgDn or PgUp

Correcting Mistakes

If you want to change only a few characters at a time, use these techniques:

- Press **Backspace** to delete the character to the left of the insertion point.

- Press Del to delete the character to the right of the insertion point.

To change more than a few characters at a time, select the text to be changed first.

The easiest way to select text is to highlight it by dragging across it with the mouse. You can double-click on a word to select it, or click at the beginning of what you want to select; then press the Shift key and click at the end of the selection. This is called **shift-clicking**, and it's a handy way of making large selections, because you can even scroll through a document as long as you remember to keep the Shift key down.

Selecting Text

❗ *Shift-click to make large selections.*

You can use the following key combinations if you want to keep your hands on the keyboard. First, make sure the insertion point is where you want the selection to begin.

To extend a selection	Press
To the next or previous line	Shift-Down arrow or Shift-Up arrow
To the end or beginning of the line	Shift-End or Shift-Home
Down or up one window	Shift-PgDn or Shift-PgUp
To the next or previous word	Ctrl-Shift-Right arrow or Ctrl-Shift-Left arrow
To the end or beginning of the document	Ctrl-Shift-End or Ctrl-Shift-Home

There are various other ways you can quickly select text in most Windows programs, but these are the basic ones.

Here's a Write tip: If you want to replace text with new text, don't bother to select it, delete it, and type the new text. Instead, just select it and then start typing. The selected text disappears, and the new text is inserted.

❗ *Quick deleting and replacing*

Chapter 3

Switching between Programs

There are three basic ways to switch between programs:

- Click in the window that's running the program you want, or double-click on its icon on the desktop, if it's been minimized.

- Bring up the Task list (press Ctrl-Esc or double-click on the desktop) and double-click on the program's name. (Or you can choose Switch To, but that's just one extra step.)

> *Pressing Alt-Esc will cycle you through all your running programs.*

- Press Alt-Esc to cycle among all the programs you've got running, including the Program Manager and any non-Windows programs. Stop when the program you want is active.

If you're running a non-Windows program in full-screen mode, when you press Alt-Esc, you'll see your program as an icon at the bottom of the screen. It will have the DOS icon, no matter what icon you've assigned to it (the chapter on customizing Windows will tell you how to assign icons to your non-Windows programs.)

> *Where you double-click makes a difference.*

Double-clicking on a program's icon on the desktop isn't the same as double-clicking on its icon in the one of Program Manager's windows. If an icon's out on the desktop, the program is really "open"—its window has been minimized—and double-clicking on it just opens it again. If you double-click on an icon in the Program Manager, you start a **new copy** of the program running, and it won't have the document you've been working with.

If the program you want to switch to hasn't been started yet, it won't be in a window. Here's a tip for starting it quickly (if it's part of a group). Bring up the Task List with Ctrl-Esc, double-click on the Program Manager, click on its Window menu, and -click on the name of the group the program is in. You can then double-click on the program to start it. For example, to start the File Manager, press Ctrl-Esc, double-click on Program Manager, click on Window, double-click on Main Group, and (finally) double-click on the File Manager's icon.

Working with Programs

Leaving Windows

When you're ready to leave Windows, you quit by exiting from the Program Manager. The fastest ways to do this are either to double-click on the Program Manager's Control icon in the upper-left corner of its window or press Alt-F4 when the Program Manager's active.

Another quick way to exit Windows is to bring up the Task List, highlight the Program Manager's name, and click End Task. (You can also choose Exit Windows from the File menu, but the other ways are faster.)

If you try to leave Windows with a non-Windows program running, you'll be asked to exit from it first. If you go back to its window to quit and accidentally press the mouse button, you'll get that pesky "Select" message. Remember, just press Esc or click the right mouse button to muzzle it. Then go back and exit from Windows.

 *Quit your non-Windows programs normally. You may need to type **exit** at the DOS prompt to exit from some non-Windows programs.*

If you've edited a document but haven't saved it, you'll also get a chance to do that before you exit Windows.

If you want to save the arrangement of the group windows and icons you were working with, click the **Save Changes** check box, or make sure that an X is already in it, as you leave Windows

Quick Tips

Here's a quick rundown of the techniques you've seen in this chapter.

Here's How To...

Start a program	Double-click on its icon.
	Press Enter when the icon is highlighted.
	Choose Run from the Program Manager's or File Manager's File menu.
	Double-click on the DOS Prompt icon and use DOS.
Start a new document	Choose New from a File menu (or press Alt-F and type N).

Here's How To...(continued)

Open a document	Choose Open from a File menu (or press Alt-F and type O).
Save a new document	Choose Save As from a File menu (or press Alt-F and type A).
Save a document	Choose Save from a File menu (or press Alt-F and type S)
Undo what you did	Choose Undo from an Edit menu (or press Alt-Backspace).
Cut	Select; then choose Cut from an Edit menu (or press Shift-Del).
Copy	Select; then choose Copy from an Edit menu (or press Ctrl-Ins).
Paste	Select; then choose Paste from an Edit menu (or press Shift-Ins).
Copy the contents of the screen	Press Print Screen (or PrtSc).
See what's on the Clipboard	Double-click on its icon.
Delete a character	Press Backspace or Del.
Select a word	Double-click on it.
Select several lines	Click at the beginning, press Shift, and click at the end.
Switch between programs	Click in the program's window, or double-click on its icon, or choose Switch To from the Task List, or press Alt-Esc to cycle among all the programs that are running.
Leave Windows	Exit from the Program Manager (double-click on its Control icon or press Alt-F4).

4

THE PROGRAM MANAGER

Central to Windows is the **Program Manager**. It comes up when you first start Windows, unless you've set up Windows so that something else will come up first. You use it to start programs and to exit Windows—in fact, you can't exit from the Program Manager without leaving Windows, too.

Besides running the whole show, the Program Manager is also a valuable tool that you can use to organize your work into groups of programs and documents that you use frequently. Once you've done that, you can easily find the icon representing what you need to work with, click a couple of times, and start working. No more "What was the name of that document?" and "Where did I save it?" or "What command do I use to start this program?"

As you saw briefly in Chapter 1, the Program Manager comes with three groups already set up for you: the Main group, the Accessories group, and the Games group.

The Program Manager

The **Main group** contains the File Manager, Control Panel, Print Manager, Clipboard, DOS Prompt, and Windows Setup programs. The File Manager, Control Panel, and the Print Manager are so important that they'll be discussed in separate chapters.

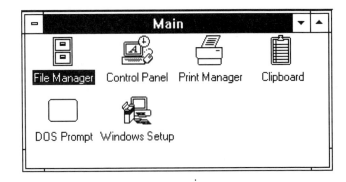

39

Chapter 4

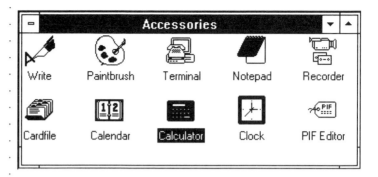

The **Accessories** are a standard or scientific calculator, a daily and monthly calendar with an alarm, a Rolodex-type cardfile, an analog or digital clock, an easy word processor called the Notepad, a fairly sophisticated painting and drawing program called Paintbrush, a Program Information File (PIF) editor for setting up information about non-Windows programs, a macro recorder, a communications program called Terminal, and Windows Write, a word processing program. The **Games** group, well...surely you've looked at it already.

In addition to these groups, you may have a **Windows Applications** group and a **Non-Windows Applications** group, if you let Windows do the walking for you during installation.

Working with the Program Manager

Program Manager

The Program Manager takes up a lot of real estate on your desktop. You can fix it so that it runs as an icon, out of your way when you're not using it. Choose Options from its menu bar; then choose **Minimize on Use**. When you start another program, the Program Manager will politely get out of your way.

The Program Manager is just a little different from other Windows programs. For one thing, it has group icons and group windows. **Group windows** are the Program Manager's windows, like the Accessories and Main groups. They contain icons that, if you double-click on them, will start programs and open documents. **Group**

The Program Manager

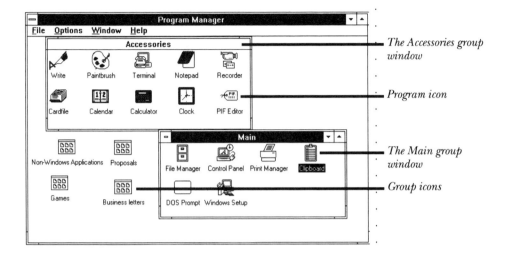

The Accessories group window

Program icon

The Main group window

Group icons

icons are simply group windows that have been minimized.

The important thing to remember about group windows is that they don't close like other windows. In fact, they don't close at all: they become icons. If you double-click on a group window's Control menu to close it (or press Ctrl-F4, which is a keyboard shortcut), it will shrink down to an icon.

If you double-click on a group window's title bar, you'll maximize the window.

You can't move a group icon out to your desktop. If you try to drag it, it becomes a "No way!" symbol. If you want to get one of the programs that's in a group out to the desktop so that you can find it easily, double-click on it; then minimize it.

To have the Program Manager always neatly arrange icons in a group window, choose Auto Arrange from the Options menu.

The Program Manager has a handy **Window menu** that lists all the groups that have been created. (It's handy because it lets you switch between groups without having

Group Windows and Icons

Business letters

 Neat trick: Double-click on an icon in a group; then minimize it to make it an icon on the desktop.

The Window Menu

CHAPTER 4

```
Window
  Cascade              Shift+F5
  Tile                 Shift+F4
  Arrange Icons

  1 Business letters
  2 Games
  3 Non-Windows Applications
√ 4 Accessories
  5 Main
```

to cycle through all the opened windows on your desktop.) The active group will have a check mark next to its name. To make a different group active, just click on its name. This will also bring that group window to the front of the stack, so if you have a lot of windows open on your desktop, it's a neat trick for finding the group you're looking for.

Creating Your Own Groups

You'll probably find that organizing programs and documents that you work with frequently into groups makes them easier to find and use. What kind of groups should you create? Well, that's up to you. You could keep your spreadsheet program in a group along with budgets you use often, or you could keep your word processing program in a group with the documents you work with most frequently, you could organize your work by project and keep all the programs you work with daily and all the documents you have to deal with in one group. Just because you put a program or a document into a group doesn't mean that you can't start the program or work with the document from somewhere other than the Program Manager. Not at all. In fact, you can start programs and open documents from the File Manager, or from the DOS prompt, just like always. Putting a program in a group just gives you a new way to start it.

Creating a New Group

To create a group of your own, choose **New** from the Program Manager's File menu. You might think this lets you start a new document, but it doesn't. Instead, you'll see the **New Program Object** dialog box.

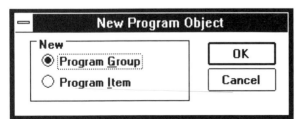

Click on the Program Group button, since you're creating a new program; then click OK (or just press Enter). You'll

42

then see the **Program Group Properties** dialog box. Enter a description (remember, this description will appear on the screen). If you've been using DOS, you've had a lot of practice at writing short, pithy descriptions for file names. You don't have to be *that* terse here. You can even use whole words! And spaces! If your descriptions get so long that they overlap on the screen, just space your icons farther apart. See Chapter 6 for how.

Leave the Group File box blank (Windows will fill it out for you); just click OK when you're done with the description.

The group window you've created will be open. You can now add programs and documents to it.

The easiest way to put a program in a group is just to move or copy its icon from another group. (If it doesn't have an icon, see "Adding Programs with Windows Setup" later in this chapter.)

To move a program icon to another group window, just drag it. To copy a program icon, press Ctrl and drag it. You can make a copy in the same group window, or in a different group window.

Here's a tip: If you use an accessory program like the Calculator or Calendar or Cardfile a lot, you can make it a part of a group. Just copy the icon into the group.

To delete a program icon, click on it to highlight it; then choose Delete from the File menu. You'll be asked to confirm that this is really what you want to do.

Deleting a program icon doesn't remove the program from your hard disk! The only way to do that is to use the File Manager's Delete command, or the DOS DEL or ERAse commands.

Adding a Program to a Group

Drag to move; Ctrl-drag to copy.

You can copy accessories, too.

Chapter 4

Another way to add a program to your new group is to choose New again from the Program Manager's File menu. This time, select **Program Item** from the New Program Object dialog box and click OK. (It may be already selected for you.) You'll see the Program Item Properties dialog box.

In the **Description** box, type the description you want to appear under the item's icon. If you're planning to include a document with this program item (more on that soon), it's a good idea to use the document's name as a part of the description. In the **Command Line** box,

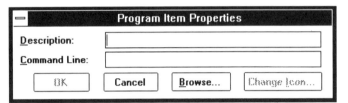

you'll need to put the information telling Windows where to find the program and what command to use to run it. There's an easy way to do this: click **Browse** to see all the executable (program) files in the current directory. Then just double-click on the name of the program you want to add, such as write.exe for Windows Write. Windows will add its path and the command that starts it to the Command Line box.

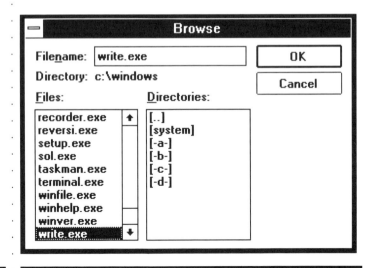

If the program you want to add isn't in the current directory, you can change directories by clicking in the Directories box. To go to a higher-level directory, click on the [..] in the Directories box.

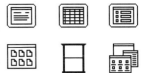 *Click on [..] to go up one level.*

Windows will automatically assign an icon to the program you've added to the group. Sometimes more than one icon is available for a program, especially if it's a non-Windows program that hasn't had an icon assigned to it. Click on **Change Icon** and **View Next** to see if you'd rather have a different icon for the program. Here are some different icons that you may be able to choose.

Changing the Icon

If you want to include a document with a program, you can do that, too. Then, when you click on the program icon, you start the program and open the document at the same time.

Adding a Document to a Group

To include a document with a program icon, just include the name of the document (and the path to it, if it isn't in the same directory as the program) at the end of the Command Line in the Program Item Properties dialog box. For example, if you'd like the Windows Write program icon to open a document called JONES.WRI when you double-click on it, type a space at the end of the command line and then type *jones.wri*. If for some reason jones.wri isn't in the directory where Windows Write is, type the path to where it is. The dialog box would look like this, if JONES.WRI were in a subdirectory called DOCS under the WINDOWS directory:

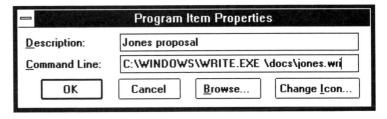

You can put several documents in a group (but no more than 40 items per group, says Microsoft!), but only one document can be included with each program icon. The program will be represented by the same icon, even if it has different documents associated with it. Be sure to use

Chapter 4

Jones proposal

a descriptive name for each one so that you can tell which is which, like this Windows Write icon named "Jones proposal." Try choosing different icons if you have a lot of program-plus-a-document icons in a group.

> If you want to put several documents in a group, make several copies of the icon of the program used to run them (press Ctrl and drag to copy icons on the same disk.) Then set each one up to open a different document.

Your non-Windows program must be able to start and open a document at the same time if you want to do this.

> This is a handy way to get around the limitations of your favorite non-Windows program that only lets you work with only document at a time. Just run several copies of it, each with its own document, and switch between them. You can use the Clipboard to transfer text between them, as you saw in Chapter 3.

When you start the program from its icon, you're in effect starting another copy of the program. It's possible that you could run out of memory if you start enough different copies of a large program. If that happens, you'll have to exit from a few of them (see the "Oh, No!" chapter for troubleshooting tips).

> Non-Windows programs are all represented by that same DOS icon when they're minimized (out on the desktop), even if you assigned them different icons in the Program Manager. If you're running several copies of the same program (and haven't used different descriptions for them), here's how to tell them apart. Look very closely. Next to the second one's name, there'll be a tiny dot. Next to the third copy, there'll be two tiny dots, and so forth. This may help you keep track of which one's which. A better way is to tile their windows, if you can, so that you can see what's in each one. But since you can't run some non-Windows in anything less than full-screen size, use this tip to keep track of their icons.

WordPerfect WordPerfect·

Adding Programs with Windows Setup

A quick way to add several programs to groups at the same time is to use the Windows Setup utility program. You may want to do this if you've run out and bought a bunch of new Windows programs after installing Windows. It's in the Program Manager's Main group.

Windows Setup

To start Windows Setup, double-click on its icon. You'll see a screen listing particulars about your hardware—what kind of display you're using, the keyboard and mouse you have, and so forth. Choose Set Up Applications from the Options menu that's part of this screen.

You'll then see the Set Up Applications dialog box. Choose whether you want to search all your drives or just specific ones (by clicking on the arrow), or whether you want to search only one directory path. Click OK to start the search.

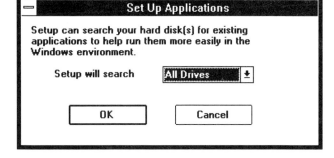

Windows will search whatever you told it to search. When it's done, you'll see the programs it found listed on the left. Highlight any you want to make into Program Manager group icons (you can click on more than one, or choose Select All to select all of them) and then click OK. Windows will (usually) figure out which are Windows programs and which aren't and will put them into either the Windows Applications group or the Non-Windows Applications group. You can move them into other groups later.

Chapter 4

> Setup isn't always good at figuring out anything except Windows programs and most of the popular non-Windows programs. If you run Setup and find out that it didn't set up a program you want to add, see the "Oh, No!" chapter.

> There's also a way to use the File Manager to put programs in groups. You'll see it in the File Manager chapter.

Changing a Group's Name

If you want to change a group's name, click its icon. Then choose File and then Properties. Type a new name and click OK. That's it.

Deleting a Group

At some point you'll probably decide that you'd like to get rid of some of your groups. To delete a group, click on its icon and then choose Delete from the Program Manager's File menu. You'll be asked to confirm that that's really what you want to do. You delete group icons and program item icons the same way.

Deleting an icon doesn't delete the program! It's still on your hard disk.

Running Programs from the Program Manager

Here's a brief rundown of how to run programs from the Program Manager.

Double-click on an icon to start the program and open any document that you've included with it. (The program has to have been added to the group before you can start it.)

> There's another way to have Windows open documents and start programs at the same time. You can *associate* documents that have the same extension with specific programs. You'll see how in the File Manager chapter.

To start a program from the DOS prompt, click on the DOS Prompt icon (it's in the Main group) and then use the DOS command line as you normally would. This is a good way to start programs that you hardly ever use and don't want to bother making a part of a group. When you're done, type *exit* at the DOS prompt to return to Windows.

THE PROGRAM MANAGER

Program Manager's Keyboard Shortcuts

Here's a summary of the keyboard shortcuts you can use with the Program Manager:

To	Use
Get help on the Program Manager	Alt-H
Get the help index	F1
Tile group windows	Shift-F4
Cascade group windows	Shift-F5
Move to another selection in the same window	Arrow keys
Move between group windows	Ctrl-F6 or Ctrl-Tab
Close a group window	Ctrl-F4
Exit from the Program Manager (Windows)	Alt-F4

Quick Tips

Here's a quick rundown of the techniques you saw in this chapter:

Here's How To...

Shrink a group window to an icon	Double-click on its Control menu or click on its Minimize icon.
Maximize a group window	Double-click on its title bar or click on its Maximize icon.
Create a new group	Choose New from the Program Manager's File menu; click Program Group; fill out a description and a command line.
Add an item to a group	Copy or move the program's icon into the group (press Ctrl and drag to copy it; drag to move it). Or choose New from the Program Manager's File menu; click Program Item; fill out a description and a command line.

Chapter 4

Here's How To...(continued)

Change an item's icon	Choose Change Icon and View Next in the Program Item Properties dialog box.
Add a document to a program item	Add the document's name to the end of the command line in the Program Item Properties dialog box.
Change a group's name	Click its icon; choose File and then Properties.
Delete a group	Click its icon; choose File and Delete.
Add a program via Setup	Double-click on the Setup icon; choose Options and then Set Up Applications. Pick which drive or directory to search; click on the program you want to add, and then click OK.
Move a program icon to another group	Drag it.
Copy a program to another group icon	Press Ctrl and drag it.
Run a program from the Program Manager	Double-click on its icon.

5

THE FILE MANAGER

The File Manager is Windows' utility for letting you do your computer "housekeeping"—moving files around, viewing what's stored on a disk, locating a particular file, and so forth. It's a big improvement over the way DOS made you do these things. Instead of copying files by using cryptic commands, for example, you can just drag their icons.

We're not going to look at everything the File Manager can do, or you'd be in this chapter for the rest of the day! We'll just examine the things you'll probably do most often.

But before you begin to look at the File Manager, it's important that you understand at least a little bit of how DOS organizes your files behind the scenes. Windows does a pretty good job of keeping you away from DOS, but you still need some idea of how its system of files and directories works, so that you can *find things*.

If you're already familiar with files, directories, and paths, just skip to later in the chapter.

Files and Directories

Each document you create and save is stored as a **file**. There are different kinds of files.

Program files have a .COM or .EXE after them, like windows.exe. (These three characters are called an *extension* because they're an addition to the file name. They can help identify what kind of file it is.) Files like these are executable programs. You can run the program, but you can't see what's inside the file.

Document files can contain text, graphics, spreadsheet data, or what have you. These are the files you create by using programs. They may have all sorts of extensions, like .TXT for a Notepad file, .XLS for an Excel spreadsheet, or even no extension at all. WordPerfect, for example, doesn't use any extension.

There are also **other files** that certain programs need, like printer and system files. These, too, have all sorts of extensions. You usually can't see what's in them. If you see anything, it'll be garbage.

Naming Files

Use a maximum of eight characters.

DOS (and therefore Windows) is pretty rigid when it comes to letting you name files. Unlike naming icons, where you can use whole words with spaces between them, you can only use **eight characters** for file names. (Plus that three-character extension, but most Windows programs will add that for you automatically.)

Forbidden Characters

There are some characters you can't ever use in file names:

<> angle brackets

\ backslash

| bar

[] brackets (either one)

: colon

, comma

= equals

+ plus sign

" quotation mark

; semicolon

/ slash

If you use a period, DOS will think it's the beginning of the extension, so be careful and only use a period there and nowhere else.

You can use some other symbols, though: $ ~ # @ ! ' ( ) { } - _ and ^ are all acceptable. They can help you give a more descriptive name to a file, such as 10-28LTR for a letter you wrote on October 28.

These are all acceptable file names:

BOB_2.WRI, SUE-1.TXT, LTR#3

These are not:

BOB/2.WRI, SUE+1.TXT, LTR*3

DOS converts everything to uppercase letters, so just type away in lowercase; it doesn't matter.

Popular Extensions

Windows automatically assigns extensions to many of the files you create, depending on which Windows program you're in. Here are some of these so that you can identify which program they belong to:

.BMP   Paintbrush graphic
.CAL   Calendar file
.CLP   Clipboard file
.CRD   Card file
.INI   Windows settings files
.MSP   Paintbrush graphic (older version)
.PCX   PC Paintbrush graphic
.PIF   Program Information File
.TXT   Notepad file
.WRI   Windows Write file

Here are some extensions other popular programs use:

.WKS   Lotus 1-2-3
.XLS   Excel
.WSD   WordStar
.DBF   dBASE

Naming Your Files

Using only eight characters to name all your files means that you've got to be pretty creative. The best thing to do is set up a system and follow it rigidly. For example, you might decide to name all your letter files like this: 10-2LET. This would mean (to you) that the file is a business letter written on October 2. A letter written on November 13 would be 11-14LET.

You may not want to use the date, because you can use Windows to see the date the file was last changed (more on this later). Instead, you might organize files by project, or by client, or by type of file (report, budget, and so forth). As long as you use a consistent naming system, it'll be easy to locate the file you're looking for. But if you get sloppy and start naming a few documents TIM_LET or QUOTE, you've blown your system and may have trouble finding what you're looking for. Set up a system. Be consistent.

Directories On your computer, files are organized into a system of **directories**. Think of a directory as a file folder in your filing cabinet. You can put all kinds of things in a directory—programs, different documents, graphics, whatever you like. Directories can even hold directories, which are called **subdirectories**, just as you stuff folders inside other folders in a filing cabinet.

The Root Directory At the very beginning of your directory system is what DOS calls the **root directory**. All the directories and subdirectories branch off from it. Everybody says it's like a **tree** and its branches, but it's not: it's like an *upside-down* tree and its branches. The root is on top, folks. (This is somewhat typical of DOS thinking.)

 When you start your computer and get that **C:\>** prompt, you're at the root directory. The C: indicates that you're on drive C, which is usually the name of your hard drive. It may be D: or E:, depending on your computer, but A: and B: are usually floppy disk drives. The \ indicates the root directory. That's why you can't use it in a file name.

If you've never ever created any directories before, all of your files will be in the root directory, except for your Windows files and maybe your DOS files. They'll be in directories named C:\WINDOWS and C:\DOS, which were created when you installed them. It's really much easier in the long run to use a more organized filing system. The File Manager can help you set yourself up a system of directories and subdirectories.

While you've been using Windows, you've probably seen the **[..]** symbol—when you've browsed for files, for example. Clicking on this symbol will back you up one level of directories toward the root directory. If you keep clicking on [..], you'll eventually wind up at the root directory.

At this point, you're probably wondering how DOS (and you) can keep track of where things are, if you've got subdirectories within subdirectories within subdirectories. Well, that's where the **path** comes in. The path is just a list of all the directories that lead to the directory that contains the file that you're looking for, like the house that Jack built. What's confusing about the path is the cryptic notation you use to write it out. You separate each directory with a backslash, so C:\WINDOWS\WRITE is the path to a subdirectory named WRITE under the WINDOWS directory on drive C:.

The Path

When you use the File Manager, you can get a graphic representation of where your directories are and what's in them, so you won't have to worry about paths very often. But you do have to use them sometimes in the File Manager, so remember that you read about it here.

DOS is automatically told the path to your Windows directory when you install Windows.

Finally, the File Manager! But, believe me, you need to know the preceding stuff so you won't get lost.

The File Manager is in the Main group, although you might expect that it would be right out there with the Program Manager. Well, the File Manager is a little different, and it works in just a little different way.... You'll see.

The File Manager

File Manager

The Directory Tree

When you double-click on the filing cabinet icon, you'll see the File Manager's screen. It will be showing a window called the **Directory Tree**. (Yours will look different, of course, since it will show the directories on your computer).

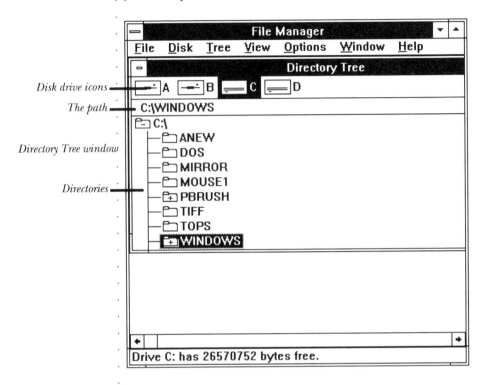

Disk drive icons
The path
Directory Tree window
Directories

At the top of the screen, all the disk drives on your computer will be represented by little drive icons. This one's got four: A: are B: and floppy disk drives, and C: and D: are hard drives. It's showing what's on the C: drive. (If you're on a network, you'll see slightly different icons for network drives.) To change to another drive, click on the icon for that drive. You'll see another Directory Tree window showing what's on that drive.

The C:\ immediately under the drive icons indicates that you're looking at the root directory of drive C:. If you click on one of the directory folders, you'll see this line change, and the notation will be just like you saw earlier when we talked about what a path was. Each directory name will be separated by a backslash.

Directories are represented by tiny file folder icons. If you look closely, you'll see that the Windows directory has a + on it. This means that there are subdirectories, which Windows calls **subtrees**, underneath it.

Seeing the Directory Structure

You can click on a directory icon that has a + on it to see the subdirectories (subtrees) that are in it.

To see your whole directory structure, choose Expand All from the File Manager's Tree menu. You'll then see a graphical representation of how your directories are structured. When you do this, all the directories that had a + on them will be opened up to show what's in them. The + will change to a -, indicating that the directory has been **expanded**. (A + on a directory means that it's **collapsed**.)

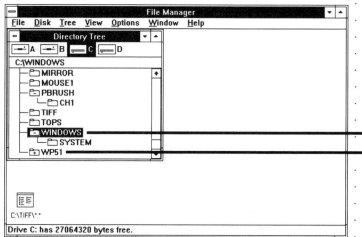

Expanded directory
Collapsed directory

Expanding and Collapsing Directories

Here are a few shortcuts for expanding and collapsing directories. Press

+   To expand a selected directory one level (assuming it's got a + on it)

*   To expand all the selected directory's subdirectories

If you double-click (instead of just click) on a directory icon that has a + on it, you'll see all the files in it instead of expanding it to see its subdirectories.

Chapter 5

● *You can use the /, *, -, and + keys on the numeric keypad; they're called Gray keys.*

Ctrl-Gray* To expand all the subdirectories of all of the directories

– To collapse the directory (assuming it's got a - on it)

You can use the Tree menu's Expand One Level, Expand Branch, Expand All, or Collapse Branch commands if you forget what these shortcuts are.

● To collapse the whole directory display, just click on the root directory's icon (the one at the very top of the display).

● *Lost the File Manager?*

If you're looking for the File Manager after you've started it, press Ctrl-Esc to bring up the Task List; then double-click on File Manager. If you double-click on the File Manager's icon in the Main group, you'll just get a "File Manager is already running" message, which isn't much help in letting you find it.

Looking in a Directory

● *Directory Tree windows and directory windows are different.*

If you double-click on a directory icon or press Enter when the directory name is highlighted, you'll see what's in the directory. This is called a **directory window**. If a lot of files are in there, you'll have to scroll, probably both horizontally and vertically, to see them all.

Maximize a directory window to see more of what's in it.

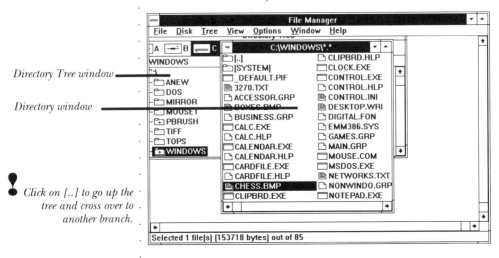

Directory Tree window

Directory window

● *Click on [..] to go up the tree and cross over to another branch.*

THE FILE MANAGER

The files with the little icons with a bar across the top are program files. If you double-click on one of them, you'll start the program it represents.

Those that have lines across them are files that have been associated with a program. (You'll see how to associate files and programs later.) If you double-click on one of them, you'll start the program that it belongs to as well as open the document.

Those without lines that have one corner turned down are other files—dog-eared, as some people call them—are files that your program needs, or files that haven't been associated with a program yet. You'll just get an error message if you double-click on any of these icons.

📄 **BOXES.BMP** —— *Associated document file*
🗋 **BUSINESS.GRP** — *Other file*
☐ **CALC.EXE** —— *Program file*

File Manager Icons

If what you're looking for in a directory window (one that shows files) is a subdirectory under another directory on a different branch, you'll have to go back toward the root and switch over to the other branch. Think about it for a minute. You're in a directory named C:\WINDOWS\LETTERS and you want to go to a directory named C:\WORD\REPORTS:

```
        C: (your root directory)
        |                |
      WINDOWS          WORD
      LETTERS          REPORTS
```

You can't just cross over to the other branch; you have to go back up to the root directory (C:\) and then go down to \WORD\REPORTS. (Or you can go back to the Directory Tree window and click on the directory icons.)

Click on [..] to go up one level. The [..] is the first item in a directory window, and you can press Home to move to it quickly. Depending on where you are in your directory structure, you may have to click on [..] more than once to reach the root directory. Once you're there, you can move down another branch.

Climbing the Branches in a Directory Window

❗ *In a Directory Tree window, you can just double-click on a directory to see what's in it.*

❗ *If there's a file you use frequently but have to scroll to find, rename it so that it begins with a number. Then it'll appear near the beginning of the directory listing.*

59

Chapter 5

Managing Directory Windows

The File Manager lets you open directory windows to your heart's content. You can even open several different windows of the same directory, showing exactly the same thing. The File Manager doesn't care. It just helpfully keeps opening windows each time you double-click on a directory icon. This can create a very cluttered screen as you search for the files you're looking for. Here are some tricks for dealing with the File Manager's windows. You may want to skim them now and refer to them later, when you get frustrated with the File Manager.

Replace Window Contents

Instead of having the File Manager open a new directory window each time you click on another subdirectory, choose **Replace on Open** from the View menu. Instead of cluttering up your screen with windows, the File Manager will just replace the contents of the next directory in the window you've already got open. If you're not going to copy or move files between directories, this is a much less confusing way to view your files.

Cycle Windows

Cycle through directory windows with Ctrl-Tab or Ctrl-F6.

To cycle through all the open directory windows, keep on pressing **Ctrl-Tab**. (They're really document windows.) You can tile them by pressing **Shift-F4**, or cascade them with **Shift-F5**. If you need to arrange directory windows side by side, tile them so that you can see a little of what's in each one. You can then arrange the ones you want next to each other by dragging them by their title bars.

Minimize Windows

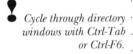

If you find that you're using one directory window over and over, **minimize** it while you're not using it! It will appear out on the File Manager's screen, where you can get at it again easily by double-clicking on it. To minimize a directory window, click its Minimize icon.

Use the Window Menu

If you minimize a directory window, it won't go zipping out to the desktop like a group window will in the Program Manager. It will still be at the bottom of the File Manager's window, and you may have to move or resize some other File Manager windows to find it. A quicker way is to use the **Window menu**. It will list all the directory windows you've got open (minimized is still

THE FILE MANAGER

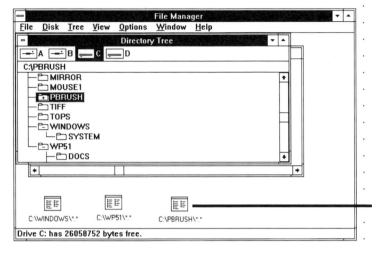

Minimized directory window

"open") and you can click on the name of the one you're looking for.

The Window menu also has a handy Close All Directories command that cleans up your File Manager screen very quickly by closing all the directory windows you've opened.

You can't close a Directory Tree window by closing all the directory windows or by double-clicking on its Control menu icon. (This is one of the ways the File Manager is different from the Program Manager.) Even if you open the Control menu, you'll see that the Close option is gray, which means you can't use it. The Directory Tree window will remain open as long as you're using the File Manager. (You can minimize it, though.) To close it, you have to exit from the File Manager. You can double-click on the File Manager's Control menu icon, or choose Exit from the File menu, or end its task on the Task List. You won't leave Windows, like you do when you exit from the Program Manager.

If you're planning to work with the File Manager again soon, don't close it. Just minimize it. It'll be easier to find later.

Closing Windows

❗ *The Directory Tree window doesn't close until you exit from the File Manager.*

❗ *Minimize the File Manager instead of closing it.*

61

Chapter 5

Saving Settings   If you check the Save Settings box when you exit from the File Manager, you expect that all your directory windows will be arranged the same the next time you start, right? Wrong. Checking the File Manager's **Save Settings** box just saves the settings you changed on the Options and View menus (as you'll see later), so you'll see your files displayed as you specified, but just the Directory Tree will come up next time.

Selecting Files and Directories   The File Manager simplifies your work with routine file management chores like moving, copying, and renaming. But before you can move or copy files and directories, you'll need to **select** them. Usually, you just click on the one you want.

❗ *Ctrl-click or Shift-click to select several files. To select several groups of files, Shift-click to select the first group. Then press Ctrl and click to select the first file in the second group. Then press Shift and Ctrl and click on the last file in the second group,. Repeat Ctrl-click and Shift-Ctrl-click as needed to add groups.*

To select more than one file, if they're next to each other, use the Shift-click method: Click on the first one; then press Shift, hold it down, and click on the last one. If they're not next to each other, press Ctrl and click on each one.

❗ *Quick selecting: Type the first letter of the file's name. This will work with either directory names or file names.*

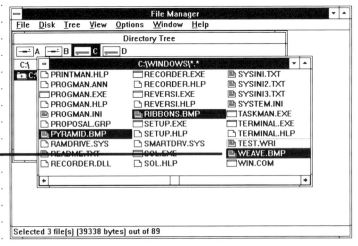

Ctrl-click to select nonadjacent files

❗ *To deselect one file, press Ctrl and click on it. To deselect all but one file, click on that file.*

If you don't have a mouse, you'll go nuts. Here are a few ways to use the keyboard. They work fine as shortcuts, but you wouldn't want to have to do this all the time!

62

The File Manager

To	Press
Select a file	Type the first letter of its name to go to that part of the alphabetical listing
Select adjacent files	Shift-arrow keys (Mouse: Shift-click)
Select nonadjacent files	Press and release Shift-F8; then use the arrow keys to move the selection box. Press the space bar to select. (Mouse: Ctrl-click)
Ctrl-/	Select all files
Ctrl-\	Deselect all files

❗ *Before you can copy or move a file, you have to select it.*

❗ *There's also a Select All Files and Deselect All Files command on the File menu.*

You'll often want to **copy** files or **move** them to new locations. Windows definitely makes this easier than DOS did! To copy and move files and directories, you just drag them to where you want them. If they won't go where you want to put them, you'll be told.

Copying and Moving Files and Directories

First, arrange the screen display so that you can see both what you're copying and the window or icon of where you're copying it to. (You may want to tile the windows.) Select the file you want to copy (for several files, **Shift-click** or **Ctrl-click**). If you're copying a whole directory,

Copying

To copy to WINDOWS, press Ctrl and drag

63

Chapter 5

select its icon. If you're copying several directories, select their icons. Then drag the file or directory icons to their new destinations.

If you're copying them to new locations on the *same disk*, press Ctrl while you drag. (If you don't press Ctrl, you'll move the files instead of copying them.) If you're copying to a different disk—say, a floppy disk in drive A: —just drag.

You'll be asked to confirm what you're doing if there are duplicate file names already in the new location. If you copy a file on top of a file that has the same name, you'll overwrite what was in the old file.

A copied directory will be placed *under* the directory where you copied it.

Minimize directory icons for multiple copy jobs.

C:\WP51\MASTER*.*

If you're copying a lot of files into a lot of different directories, minimize the directories and then just drag the files onto the directory icons. This can save you a lot of window arranging.

To copy via the keyboard, use the **Copy command** on the File menu and fill out the From: and To: sections of the dialog box. Use the path for the To: destination, as it will undoubtedly be in a different directory!

If you highlight the file (or files) you want to copy first, they'll automatically be put in the From: box (it may not show them all, if you've selected a lot of them).

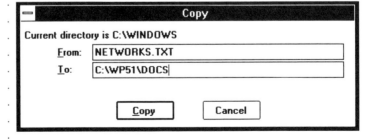

64

The File Manager

The advantage to using the Copy command instead of selecting icons and dragging them is that you can use special characters called **wildcards** to specify a lot of files that have similar names or extensions, which can save you some time. The characters ***** and **?** are called **wildcard characters**. Just like in poker, a wild card can stand for something else. The **asterisk** (*) represents any number of characters (including none at all), and the **question mark** (?) represents any one character.

For example, to copy everything ending in .XLS (Excel spreadsheets), enter *.XLS. To copy everything beginning with A and having any extension, like APRIL.WRI or AB_DOC.TXT or ACCOUNT.XLS, enter a*.*. To copy both the files BROWN.TXT and BRAUN.TXT, enter BR??N.TXT. Using wildcards can save you time, but they take a little getting used to.

You can also copy whole directories by using the Copy command. Just enter the path to the directory, like C:\WINDOWS\BUDGETS.

Moving files and directories is just like copying them, except that they don't stay in the old location as well as appearing in the new location.

To move files and directories to new locations on the *same disk*, just drag them with the mouse. To move them to a different disk, press Alt while you drag.

Here's a reminder:

Drag	To copy onto a different disk
Drag	To move on the same disk
Ctrl-drag	To copy on the same disk
Alt-drag	To move onto a different disk

You can also use the Move command from the File menu if you want to use wildcards with a bunch of files to be moved.

Wildcards

❗ *To select all the files in a directory, press Ctrl-/.*

❗ *The keyboard shortcut for Copy: F8*

Moving

❗ *The keyboard shortcut for Move: F7.*

65

CHAPTER 5

Moving Directories — If you move a directory, all of the files in it moves with it. Windows places the moved directory *under* the directory where you moved it. After you've moved a directory, it will ask you if you want to remove the original subtree (directory, which is now empty). You probably do, because it's empty, so click Yes.

Renaming Files and Directories — Easy. Select the file or directory and choose Rename from the File menu. Enter the new name in the dialog box and click OK. Just remember to follow DOS's rules. See "Naming Files" earlier in this chapter for a refresher.

Creating a New Directory — If your file system is a mess, you can use Windows to straighten it out. One of the first things you'll need to do is create some new directories so that you can organize your files in them.

Here's how to do it. Open the Directory Tree window and click on the directory that you want the new directory to be created under. You'd click on the WINDOWS directory to create a new subdirectory for it.

From the File menu, choose **Create Directory**. You'll see a dialog box where you can enter the name you want your new directory to have. Enter it and click OK. (Remember: eight characters. You can also use an extension with directory names, but few people do.) That's it. You've now got a new, empty directory, and you can put files in it. You can see it in the Directory Tree window if it's expanded.

You can create subdirectories under your new directory by highlighting it in the Directory Tree and doing the same thing over again. For example, you might want to create subdirectories for different kinds of documents under the directory that holds your word processing program. Here you can see that the WP51 directory (it holds WordPerfect 5.1) has subdirectories called MACROS, LEARN, DOCS, and MASTER, and the MASTER subdirectory has subdirectories of its own.

The File Manager

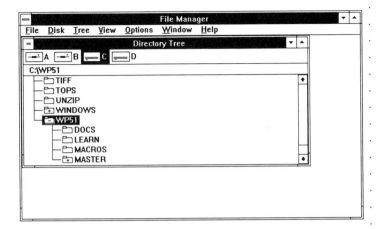

Sooner or later, you're going to want to remove a few files from your directories. But be careful: Make sure you really want to delete a file before you do it, because it's difficult (but not impossible) to get it back. You'll have to have one of the sophisticated disk utility programs like the Norton Utilities or PC Tools to recover deleted files, so the easiest thing to do is not delete files that you want to keep in the first place.

Deleting is the same as **erasing**. To delete, select the file or files you want to delete (Shift-click to select adjacent files, or Ctrl-click to select nonadjacent ones) and choose Delete from the File menu. You'll see a dialog box; double-check that the file name (or names) are the ones that you really want to delete; then click OK.

If you want to delete files that are in other directories, you can type the path to them.

You can also use wildcards to delete a bunch of files at a time, such as OCTRPT?.WRI to delete all your OCTRPT1.WRI, OCTRPT2.WRI, OCTRPT3.WRI files, and so forth.

But *be careful.* You can erase everything that's in a directory by entering *.*. You may want to do this

Deleting Files

Unlike deleting an icon, deleting a file in the File Manager really removes it from your disk.

Shift-click to select adjacent files; Ctrl-click for nonadjacent files.

67

sometimes, especially to erase everything on a used floppy disk so that you can use it again— but be sure that it's really what you want to do.

Deleting Directories Someday you'll probably want to delete a directory. The files in it may have become hopelessly outdated, for instance. The File Manager's File menu lets you delete a directory just like you delete a file.

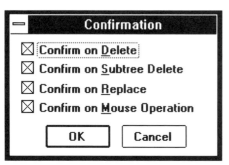

DOS was very stubborn about letting people delete directories and absolutely refused to do it unless the directory was empty. The File Manager isn't so choosy, and it will let you delete a directory full of files if you turn off your confirmation prompts by using the Options menu, choosing Confirmation, and clicking to uncheck the confirmation prompts.

Because of this "feature," make sure you keep all your confirmations checked so that you don't delete a directory full of files by mistake!

Finding Files You can spend a lot of time looking for a file. It gets worse if you're not even sure which file you're looking for. Windows has thankfully included a file-finding feature that can help you locate a file if you know its name, or even part of its name.

To search for a file, select Search from the File menu. In the dialog box that appears, type the name of the file you want to find.

If you don't know the name of what you want to search for, try using wildcards. You may know that it begins with F, so you could enter F*.* to find everything beginning with F. If you know that it has a .TXT extension, enter *.TXT to find everything ending in .TXT. The dialog box will initially be set to *.*, which means everything, and you certainly don't want to search for *everything*, so enter *something* in the box!

The File Manager

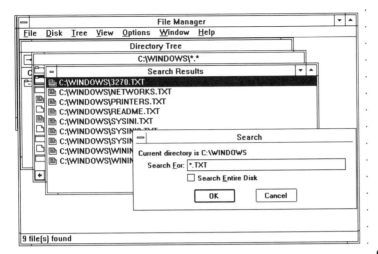

Uncheck the Search Entire Disk box if you don't want Windows to search your whole disk. If you have a large hard disk, this can take a while. With the box unchecked, Windows will search just the current directory and all its subdirectories. So if you want to search a specific directory, make it current before you use the Search command.

To quickly select a group of files that have similar names, search for them and then select them all by pressing Ctrl-/.

If you don't know anything about the file's name but do know that you created it on a certain day, don't use the Search command. Use the View menu instead. This is another way to locate files you're looking for.

Use the View menu to search by date.

You can use the File Manager's View menu and choose **View File Details** to see the date and time each file was last saved as well as the actual size of each file, in bytes.

Using the View Menu

Chapter 5

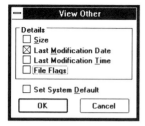

You probably don't need to see all this information all the time. It's often useful to be able to see the last date you changed a file, though. To see just this information, choose **View Other** and then just click on **Last Modification Date**. Click on the Set System Default box if you always want to see your files this way.

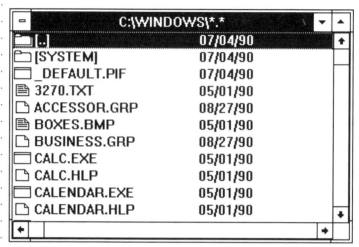

Sorting a Display You can even tell Windows to sort your files so that you can see the most recent files first. To do this, choose **Sort by Last Modification Date** from the View menu.

If this is the way you always want to see your files, click the Set System Default box.

Listing Files Alphabetically Another way of looking at files is alphabetically by file name. If you'd rather see them that way, choose **View by Name** or **Sort by Name** from the View menu.

Looking at Types of Files

If you've got a whole lot of files in a directory, you may not want to see them all. The Include command lets you just look at some kinds of files (don't you think it ought to have been called "Exclude"?) For example, if all you want to see is documents, uncheck everything but the Documents box.

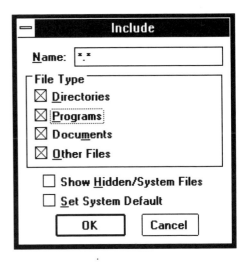

If all you want to see is document files with a certain extension—like .TXT files for the Notepad—change what's in the Name box to *.txt. The Name box usually has *.* in it. Remember, these wildcards mean "everything with any extension." You can substitute other patterns to restrict which file names will be displayed.

If you know the name of the file you're looking for but aren't quite sure how you spelled it, the ? wildcard can come in handy. Suppose you wanted to find a file named OLSON.WRI, but you weren't sure whether it was OLSON or OLSEN. Just enter *ols?n.wri*, or *ols?n.** if you're not sure of the extension.

● *Use wildcards to help you search.*

Starting Programs with the File Manager

As you saw in Chapter 3, you can also start programs by using the File Manager. This is a convenient way to start seldom-used programs that you don't want to put in a group. You saw how to use these two basic methods:

- Double-click on a program's icon.
- Use the Run command and enter the command used to start the program, including its path if necessary.

There are a couple more things you can do to start programs in the File Manager:

- Drag a document icon onto its program icon.
- Double-click on the icon of a document that's associated with a program.

If you drag a document's icon onto its program's icon,

Chapter 5

Dragging a Document Icon

that will start the program and open the document at the same time (you'll be asked to confirm that that's really what you want to do). If both aren't in the same directory, you'll need to arrange the directory windows so that you can see both the program's icon and the document's icon.

Getting these windows next to each other can be tricky, but this way usually works: Open the directory that has the document and drag its window over to the right of the screen. Then open the directory that contains the program. Click back in the window that has the document to activate it. If you still can't see the right windows, minimize everything but the File Manager; then choose Tile from the Window menu. You should be able to see a little bit of every window now, but you may have to scroll horizontally to find the right document.

Associating Documents and Programs

Unassociated documents

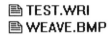

Associated documents

If a document has been **associated** with a program, its icon has little lines on it. If you double-click on one of these icons, the program that's associated with the document will start and open the document. Most of the documents created in Windows programs are automatically associated with the program that created them, so you can start Windows Write just by clicking on one of its documents, for example. You can also associate non-Windows documents with their programs, so that you can start the program by clicking on an associated document.

To associate documents with programs, they must have an extension as part of their file name. It doesn't have to be three characters—even one character will do.

What you do when you associate documents with programs is tell Windows, "Look, all the files that end in .XXX (or .XX, or .X) belong to program AAA, so start that program whenever I double-click on one of those files, OK?"

To associate documents with a program, select one of the

documents in a directory window, choose **Associate** from the File menu, and type the command used to run the program you want to associate that type of document with.

If the program's in a different directory, you'll have to indicate the path to it. For example, to associate a document named CH2.PPP with WordPerfect 5.1 in a different directory called \wp51, you would enter *c:\wp51\wp* at the " '.PPP' files are associated with:" prompt.

This is a tricky example, because if you use WordPerfect, you know that it doesn't automatically use any extensions. You have to set up a system of extensions for yourself. This .PPP is for—Peachpit Press; what else?

You only have to do this for one document; Windows automatically associates all the rest of the documents that have the same extension.

You don't have to associate documents to use the drag-an-icon technique.

You can use the File Manager to add programs to your Program Manager groups, too. Here's how to do it (you have to have a mouse).

Adding Programs with the File Manager

Open a directory window in the File Manager, next to the group window you want to add the program to. (You'll need to have created the group window first, if it doesn't already exist; see Chapter 4 for how.) Drag the icon of the program you want to add from the File Manager window to the group window you want to add it to.

After you've added an item to a group, you can choose Properties from the Program Manager's File menu and change the icon's description. If you want to include a document with the program that the icon represents, add its name to the end of the command line.

It can be tricky to get the File Manager window and the

Chapter 5

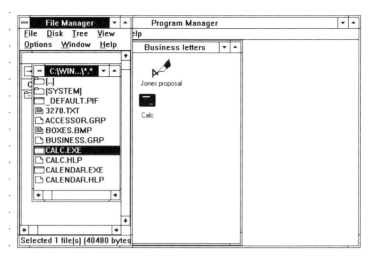

● *Lining up windows*

group window open at the same time, because when you click on a file name in the File Manager, the other windows run and hide. Here's how: Locate the program in the File Manager *first;* then bring up the Task List (you can use the old double-click-on-the-desktop trick or press Ctrl-Esc) and choose Tile to see all the other windows. (If you're running the File Manager in full-screen size, you'll need to click its Restore icon to make it smaller so that you can get out to the desktop.)

Copying Disks

What else can the File Manager do for you? Well, it also lets you **copy floppy disks** without going out to DOS. It's a little faster than using DOS. Here's how.

Put the disk you want to copy (**the source** disk) in your floppy disk drive and click on that drive's icon in the Directory Tree window. Then click on the icon of the floppy drive that's going to hold the blank disk. This is called **the destination** drive. (If you only have one floppy drive, don't worry.) Choose Copy Diskette from the Disk menu.

You'll be warned that any data on the destination disk will be destroyed. At this point, if you have only one floppy drive, you panic, because you just put the source disk in that drive. Don't worry. The drive will whir, but another dialog box will come up telling you that you should place the source disk in the drive, so it's OK because it's already there.

Windows will copy what's on the disk (as much as it can), hold it in memory, and then copy it onto the destination disk. You'll be prompted to swap disks as necessary.

Your disks have to be the same capacity for you to use windows' Copy Diskette command. If they aren't the same capacity, use the Copy command and copy *.* (everything) from one disk to another, as you saw earlier.

 Use Copy Diskette on similar-sized disks.

To check a disk's capacity, read its label. If the disk has been used before, the label may have been covered over, though. If that's the case, you can try this trick. Put the disk in your floppy drive and click on the drive's icon. Look at the **status line** at the bottom of the screen. It will show how many bytes of information are available on that disk. If the disk is blank, you can tell what its capacity is by looking at this chart:

Bytes	**Means**
368,640	It's a 360K disk (5.25"), also called double density
1,228,800	It's a 1.2 Mb disk (5.25"), also called high density
737,280	It's a 720K disk (3.5"), also called double density (these have one square hole)
1,474,560	It's a 1.4 Mb disk (3.5"), also called high density (these have two square holes)

You can also use the information on this status line to tell whether there's enough room on a floppy disk for all the files you're planning to move or copy onto it. First, select all the files you want to copy and check the status line to see the total number of bytes you're copying. Then click on the directory window for the floppy disk you want to copy to and see how many bytes on it are free.

Chapter 5

Formatting Disks

Another thing that the File Manager makes easy is **formatting floppy disks**. Instead of having to go out to DOS and do it, you can insert your blank floppy disk in drive A: (or B:) and choose Format Diskette from the Disk menu. Click OK in response to the warning (if you're sure you want to format the disk), click on the disk drive that has the disk in it (if you have only one floppy drive, you won't need to do this), and click on Format. If you're formatting a high-density disk, check the High Capacity check box.

> High density isn't the same as double density. Windows will format your disk as a double-density disk (360 K) unless you check High Capacity. High-density disks hold a lot more than the regular kind, and they cost more, too. But if you format a double-density disk as a high-density disk, it won't work right. Look at the disk label before you format a disk.

> How can you tell whether a disk needs to be formatted? If you aren't sure, the best thing to do is check to see if there's anything already on it. Put the disk in the floppy drive, close the drive door, and double-click on drive A: or B: in the Directory Tree window. If you get a "System Error: Cannot read from drive A" message, the disk probably needs to be formatted.

If the disk is empty (formatted, but blank), you'll see a message at the bottom of the window telling you that the disk has so many bytes free. In that case, it doesn't have to be formatted; you can go ahead and use it for storing files. If there's anything on the disk, you'll see what it is and can decide whether you want to keep it or not. You can just delete what's on an already formatted disk instead of formatting it all over again. (See "Deleting Files" earlier in this chapter.)

Formatting a disk will wipe out everything that's on it. Forever. If you delete a file, you can possibly recover it with a utility program.

Windows won't let you format what's on the current drive. If you've clicked on the drive A: icon in the Directory Tree window to see what's on the disk in drive A:, you've made drive A: current. Click on the drive C: icon and then format your disk in drive A:. If you don't do this, you'll get an error message when you try to format the floppy disk in drive A:.

! *You can't format a disk on the current drive.*

There are a lot of other things you can do with the File Manager, but we'll just mention a few of them here. You can explore them on your own after you've become more accustomed to Windows and to the File Manager's somewhat eccentric habits.

Other File Manager Secrets

The **Options menu** lets you change a few things about how the File Manager's window appears. You can have everything displayed in lowercase, for example, or not have the status bar appear.

Changing the Display

The File Menu also lets you change a file's **attributes**. Attributes control whether a file can be altered as well as whether it even shows up in a directory window. This is a fairly advanced topic, so we won't go into it, but here's one tip about how you can protect an important file.

Locking a File

To make sure that a file can't be deleted or changed, set its attributes to Read Only. Select the file; then choose Change Attributes from the File menu and click the Read Only box.

You can even **print** from the File Manager, as long as you're printing text-only files and not planning to switch to a different printer. (Text-only files usually have a .TXT or .ASC extension.)

Printing

This is handy for printing out the contents of text files like "readme" files that often come with programs you buy. Just click on the file name in a directory window and choose Print from the File menu.

CHAPTER 5

File Manager's Keyboard Shortcuts

Here's a summary of the keyboard shortcuts you can use with the File Manager:

To	Use
Open a directory	Enter
Expand a collapsed directory one level	+
Expand all the selected directory's subdirectories	*
Expand all the subdirectories of all of the directories	Ctrl-*
Collapse a directory	–
Move a file or directory	F7
Copy a file or directory	F8
Delete files and directories	Del
Select a file	Type the first letter of its name
Select the first file in the window	Home
Select the last file in the window	End
Select all files in a window	Ctrl-/
Deselect all files	Ctrl-\
Cascade windows	Shift-F5
Tile windows	Shift-F4
Refresh windows	F5

THE FILE MANAGER

Here's a quick rundown of the File Manager techniques you saw in this chapter.

Quick Tips

Here's How To...

Change the current drive	Click on a drive icon in the Directory Tree window.
Open a directory window	Double-click on a directory icon or press Enter when it's highlighted.
Expand a selected directory one level (if it's got a + on it)	Press +, click on it, or choose Expand One Level from the Tree menu.
Expand all the selected directory's subdirectories	Press * or choose Expand Branch from the Tree menu.
Expand all the subdirectories of all of the directories	Press Ctrl-Gray * or choose Expand All from the Tree menu.
Collapse the directory	Press – or click on it.
Collapse the display	Click on the root directory icon.
Replace the contents of each subsequent directory window instead of opening new ones	Choose Replace on Open from the View menu.
Cycle directory windows	Press Ctrl-F6 or choose Next from the Control menu.
Tile directory windows	Press Shift-F4 or choose Tile from the Window menu.
Cascade them	Press Shift-F5 or choose Cascade from Window menu.
Minimize a directory window	Click on its Minimize icon.
Close the Directory Tree window	Choose Exit from the File menu, or double-click on the File Manager's Control icon, or choose End Task for the File Manager from the Task List.
Select a file or directory	Click on it, or type the first letter of its name.

79

Chapter 5

Here's How To...*(continued)*

Select adjacent files and directories	Shift-click, or use Shift and the arrow keys.
Select nonadjacent files and directories	Alt-click, or press Shift-F8, use the arrow keys, and use the space bar to select.
Go up one level	Click on [..].
Select the first file in the window	Press Home.
Select the last file in the window	Press End.
Select all files	Ctrl-/ or choose Select All from the File menu.
Deselect all files	Ctrl-\ or choose Deselect All from the File menu.
Deselect one file	Ctrl-click on it.
Select groups of files	Shift-click to select the first group; then Ctrl-click to select the first file in the next group; then Shift-Ctrl-click on the last file in the group. Repeat Ctrl-click; Shift-Ctrl-click to add other groups to the selection.
Use wildcards	The * stands for any combination of characters, and ? stands for any one character.
Copy on the same disk	Select; then Ctrl-drag, or press F8 and use the Copy command.
Copy onto a different disk	Select; then drag, or press F8 and use the Copy command.
Move files and directories on the same disk	Select; then drag, or press F7 and use the Move command.
Move onto a different disk	Select; then Alt-drag, or press F7 and use the Move command.
Rename a file or directory	Select it; then choose Rename from the File menu.
Delete a file or directory	Select it; then choose Delete from the File menu.

Here's How To...(continued)

Create a new directory	Click on the directory you want the new one to appear *under*, then choose Create Directory from the File menu.
Search for a file	Select Search from the File menu.
Search for a file by date	Select Sort by and Modification Date from the View menu.
Change the file information display	Use the View menu.
Start a program from the File Manager	Double-click on its icon, use the Run command, drag a document icon on top of its program icon, or double-click on an associated document icon.
Associate documents	Select the document and choose Associate from the File menu; enter the command used to run the program.
Add a program to a group	Open both a File Manager window and a group window. Drag the program's icon from the File Manager to the group.
Copy floppy disks	Choose Copy Diskette from the Disk menu.
Format floppy disks	Choose Format Diskette from the Disk menu.
Alter how File Manager windows appear	Use the Options menu.
Print ASCII files on the default printer	Choose Print from the File menu.
Protect a file	Set its attribute to Read Only.

6

CUSTOMIZING WINDOWS

The **Control Panel** is where to go when you're ready to customize Windows. Here's where you change screen colors, make the mouse into a southpaw, set the date and time format, control how Windows acts with your network (if you're on one), and so forth.

Control Panel

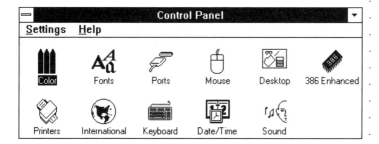

To get to the Control Panel, click on the Program Manager and then double-click on the Main group icon. When you double-click on the Control Panel icon, you'll see icons for all its utilities:

- **Color** lets you change screen colors on the desktop and in windows. If you have a color monitor, of course.

- **Fonts** lets you add or remove fonts for your printer (more about this in the printing chapter).

- **Ports** lets you tell Windows which communication ports you're using.

- **Mouse** lets you change how fast the mouse pointer moves across the screen and set the double-click interval.

The Control Panel

Chapter 6

- **Desktop** is fun; it lets you change patterns used as your desktop's background. It also lets you change the cursor's blinking rate and set up a desktop grid.

- **Printers** lets you add new printers and select the printer you want to use.

- **International** lets you use different number and currency formats, date and time formats, and so forth.

- **Keyboard** lets you adjust the rate that keys repeat when you press and hold them down.

- **Date/time** lets you rest the system's date and time.

- **Sound** just lets you turn the beep on and off. (Did you think it could make your computer play music? Sure looks like it from the icon.)

- **Network** lets you specify things about your network. You won't see this icon unless you're on a network that Windows recognizes.

- **386 Enhanced** lets you adjust how programs work with Windows in Enhanced mode. You won't see this one, either, unless you have a 386 computer.

Changing Screen Colors

If you don't have a color monitor, you can skip this part.

When you first start Windows, it comes with a color scheme already set up. It's more fun to choose one of the others, though, or create one of your own

Choosing a Color Scheme

To choose one of the other color schemes, click on the Color icon. You'll see a sample window showing which window items can be changed to colors. (You'll only see the left-hand side until you choose Color Palette.)

Press the down arrow key on the keyboard to cycle through the display of color schemes that have already been defined: Arizona (pale sand colors with blues and grays), Bordeaux (purples), Designer (gray-greens and a pattern), Fluorescent (need I say more?), monochrome (ugh), Ocean (soft blues and greens), Patchwork

CUSTOMIZING WINDOWS

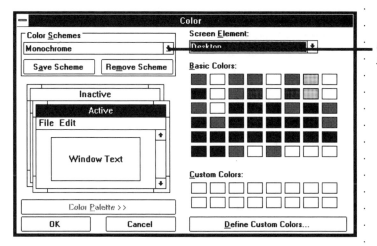

Click here to see color schemes changes

(reminiscent of a patchwork quilt, complete with dainty patterns), Rugby (maroon, blue, and yellow), Pastel (Easter egg colors), and Wingtips (browns and grays).

If you decide to use one of these, click OK (or press Enter) when it's displayed.

You can change these colors and even mix new shades of your own. First, choose one of the existing schemes that's closest to what you want. Then click on Color Palette. If you have a color monitor, you'll see an impressive array of colors and patterns. If you have a monochrome monitor, you'll see fewer colors, of course.

In the sample window on the left, click on the part you want to change, or press the down arrow when the Screen Element box is active to scroll through all the available choices. You can change the colors of the desktop, the application workspace, the window background, the window text, the menu bar and its text, the title bars (active and inactive) and title bar text, window borders (active and inactive), frames, and the scroll bars.

In the color palette part of the window, click on the color you want to use. You can choose from the basic colors or create custom colors of your own (more on this soon).

Your Own Color Scheme

85

💡 *Easy on the eyes*

Here are a few personal tips for choosing colors. Keep the type that you'll be reading in a dark color, preferably black or dark blue. Keep the background—the application workspace—a very light tint, to keep it easy on your eyes for long stretches of time. Try a light green, light blue, or light yellow.

💡 In fact, most of the other preassigned colors are probably too strong to use as a background color. If you want an easy-on-the-eyes light background, mix your own very pale shade (see below). Also keep the active title bar and the menu bar in a dark or strong color, so that you can read the words on them! If you want to use a light color there, use one with a pattern. The scroll bars and other places where you don't have to read? Go wild. Use magenta if you like, or any of the neon colors.

You can use a color scheme without saving it (just click OK or press Enter), but when you choose a different scheme, the selection of colors you chose will be lost. If you set up a combination of colors that you like, choose **Save Scheme** and type a name for the scheme. Give it a name that's different from the one it already has, so that you can tell which scheme's yours and which came with Windows.

If you create a lot of color schemes and later decide that some of them are really ugly, you can delete them with **Remove Scheme**.

Creating Custom Colors

You can "mix" 16 more custom colors and use them in your color schemes! Choose Define Custom Colors, and you'll see the Custom Color Selector dialog box. Wow! This book doesn't do it justice. The color box is an array of hues from orange to yellow to blue to purple to red, going from left to right.

On this multicolored part of the screen, you'll see a small black "box"—four little black dots. That's the **color refiner cursor**. To change colors, drag that cursor until a color you like appears in the Color/Solid box. Once you've got the color you want, you can make it brighter or darker (adjust its luminosity) by dragging in the

CUSTOMIZING WINDOWS

vertical luminosity bar. You can also adjust a color by clicking on the scroll arrows next to Hue (to change the color), Sat (to change the saturation, or purity of color), and Lum (to change the color's luminosity, or brightness).

Color refiner cursor

Check your color here

As you change colors, you'll see the new color in the Color/Solid box. You can choose a solid color by clicking in the Solid part of the box. Click in the Color part of the box to choose the color pattern displayed there.

You can also change colors by typing in new values for them, or increase the amount of red, green, or blue in a color by clicking on the arrows next to the Red, Green, and Blue boxes.

Once you've created a custom color that you want to keep, select a box in the Custom Colors palette. (Windows will automatically fill these boxes from left to right if you don't select one, but you may want to group shades together.) Choose Add Colors to add the new color to the Custom Colors palette. You can then use your new color in any color scheme you like.

Windows comes with a solid pattern for the desktop background. You can change it to a pattern (the pattern will be in the same color you chose for the desktop).

Changing Desktop Patterns

Choosing a Pattern

To choose a pattern, double-click on Desktop in the Control Panel. You'll see the Desktop dialog box (next page). In the Pattern portion, click on Edit Pattern and press the down arrow key on your keyboard (or click on the down scroll arrow on the screen) to see a list of patterns. Keep typing the down arrow to see samples of all the patterns. There are quite a few. If you see one you like, click OK. Click OK again to close the dialog box.

Desktop

Chapter 6

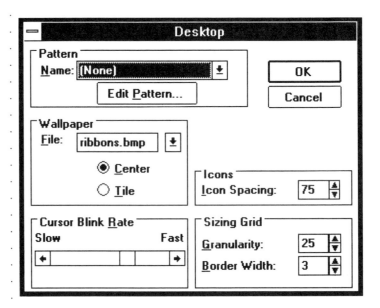

Changing a Pattern

To create a custom pattern, first choose a pattern that's close to what you want. You'll see a sample of the pattern. This one's showing the Quilt pattern. It's nice, and so is the Waffle pattern (personal favorites.)

Click on the individual bits in the pattern to change it. This is one place you have to use a mouse!

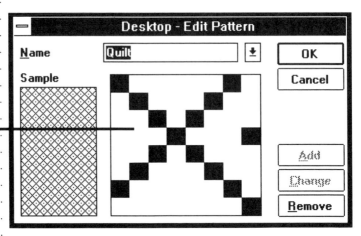

Click here to change the pattern

CUSTOMIZING WINDOWS

On the left, you'll see a sample of the pattern as it'll look on the desktop. When you've got the pattern as you like it, click Change and then OK.

When you go back to the desktop, you'll see that pattern as the desktop background. You may need to minimize some windows to see the desktop.

The pattern you've created hasn't been saved yet. The next time you start Windows, it'll be gone. If you want to save a new pattern so that you can use it again, go back to the Edit Pattern dialog box and type a new name for it in the Name box; then click Add.

Using Wallpaper

Windows comes with a collection of graphic images called **wallpaper** that you can use for your desktop. You can choose one of these, or, if you have a scanner, you can use a graphic image that you've scanned.

To choose one of Windows' wallpapers, click on the Control Panel's Desktop icon. Then click on the down scroll arrow next to the Wallpaper File box. Choose Tile to have the pattern repeat as many times as necessary to cover the whole desktop. The Chess wallpaper is big enough to cover the whole screen, but the rest have to be tiled if you want to cover all the desktop's real estate. This "paper" wallpaper has an interesting 3-D effect on the screen.

Among the other wallpapers are chess (a wild 3-D chessboard), a box pattern, a quiet pyramid pattern, and a loud party pattern. I prefer no wallpaper myself.

Click OK to see the wallpaper. If you have a lot of windows open, you may need to close them or click their

Minimize icons to get them out of the way so that you can get the wallpaper's full effect.

If you don't like any of the wallpapers, you can create your own. Windows Paintbrush saves images in bit-mapped (BMP) format, so you can use it to create your own wallpaper. You can also use Paintbrush to edit any of the wallpapers that are provided with Windows.

> If memory's a consideration for you, don't use wallpaper. It's a memory hog.

> You can't use a pattern for the desktop background and use wallpaper, too. If you've chosen both, Windows will use the wallpaper you've selected instead of the pattern as the desktop background. Set Wallpaper to None if you'd rather use a pattern.

> If you've chosen a pattern and wallpaper, Windows will use the pattern as background for text used as icon labels. This can make them pretty hard to read, if not impossible. Set Pattern to None if you'd rather use wallpaper.

Other Desktop Options You can also adjust the windows' border width, control how icons appear on the desktop, and set how fast you want the cursor to blink. Like the pattern and wallpaper options, you won't see the effects of your changes until you click OK. If you just click outside the box, no changes take place; you just make a different window active.

Icon Spacing If your icons are so close together that their names overlap, you can change the space between them by clicking on the arrows next to **Icon Spacing**. The preset value is 75 pixels (a pixel is one screen dot), but you can change it up to 512 for v-e-r-y wide spacing between icons. I keep mine around 125 so that "Non-Windows Applications," which is probably the longest group name you'll have, won't overlap with anything.

To see the effects of changing icon spacing, click OK, go to the Program Manager, and then choose Arrange Icons from the Program Manager's Window menu. (Arrange Icons only arranges the icons in the active window.)

Icon Alignment

If you're neat and orderly and you want windows to align nicely and icons to always align on an invisible grid on the desktop, choose the **Granularity** box and enter the number of pixels you want between grid lines (1 to 49), or click on the arrows to change 8 pixels at a time. To turn off the grid, enter 0. Windows comes with the grid off. I kept mine off at first but later found I liked it better with it on.

Border Width

To change the width of the borders, click on the arrows next to Border Width in the Desktop dialog box. The smallest border you can have is 1 and the widest is 49. I keep mine at 3, the default, because I like thin borders. That's what you see in the figures in this book.

You'll have to experiment with all these settings until you get them the way you like them, because you don't see the effects until you click OK to close the dialog box.

Cursor Blink

One last option in the Desktop dialog box lets you change the rate of the **cursor's blink**. Slide the scroll box in the Cursor Blink Rate box to Fast or Slow and see how fast it blinks. Click OK when the rate's as you want it.

Customizing the Keyboard

To change the rate a key repeats when you hold it down, double-click on the Keyboard icon in the Control Panel. You'll see the Keyboard dialog box.

Keyboard

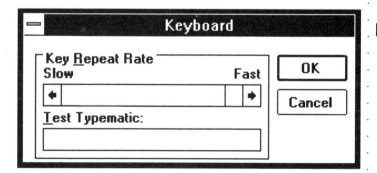

Move the box in the Key Repeat Rate to adjust the rate. Try it out by typing any key and holding it down in the Test Typematic box. Click OK to save your setting.

Customizing the Mouse

You can set the mouse's tracking and double-click speed and change it from a right-handed mouse to a left-handed one.

Mouse

When you open the Mouse icon, you'll see the Mouse dialog box. To change the **tracking speed** (the rate the mouse zips across your screen as you move it on the real desktop), drag the box in the Tracking Speed scroll bar. When you get accustomed to using the mouse, you may want to turn up the speed.

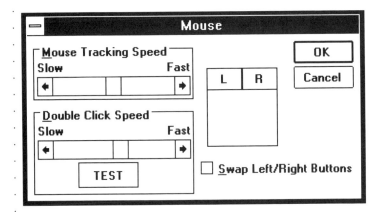

Windows interprets two "quick" clicks as a **double-click**. As you know, a double-click often produces a very different result from a single click. If your double-clicks are being interpreted as two single clicks, change the double-click response rate. You can test it out by double-clicking in the TEST box. It will change from white to black (or vice versa) when you're double-clicking fast enough for the setting you've chosen.

If you're **left-handed**, reverse the actions of the left and right mouse buttons by selecting the Swap Left Right Buttons box. Again, you can test out the new settings in the L/R box.

CUSTOMIZING WINDOWS

Remember, if you switch them, you have to switch them back by clicking with the right mouse button, not the left!

Instead of setting the date and time with the DOS DATE and TIME commands, you can double-click on the **Date/Time** icon. Just type in a new date or time, or click on the arrows to adjust the date and time shown.

Setting the Date and Time

Date/Time

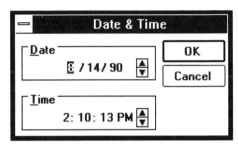

Use the International option to change the format of the date and time.

Use the **International** icon to set different formats for the date and time, currency, measurements (English or metric), and number formats. When you double-click on this icon, you'll see the International dialog box. If you're using Windows in English, you probably won't

Other Options

International

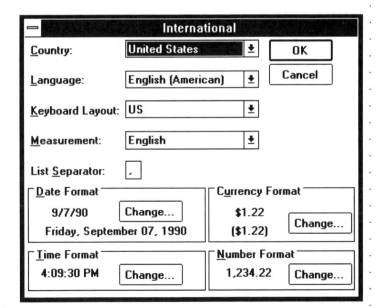

93

Chapter 6

need to change the settings, except maybe for date and time, if you want military-style dates and times, like 15 March 1991 and 23:55.

If you're running a network, you'll see a **Network** icon in the Control Panel. Use it to change your user ID, switch to a different password, and so forth. The dialog box you see will depend on the network you're connected to.

Ports

Use the **Ports** icon to specify the settings for the communications ports (COM1, COM2, and so forth) your computer uses. If you buy a modem or a serial printer (like some laser printers) or attach a serial mouse to one of these ports, you may need to change the settings. Whatever hardware you bought should have a manual with it that tells you what settings to use.

386 Enhanced

If your computer is a 386, you'll see an icon for **386 Enhanced** mode. If you're an advanced user, you can use it to fine-tune how Windows interacts with non-Windows applications and devices like printers and modems.

Customizing Help

In addition to customizing Windows with the Control Panel, you can also customize Windows **Help**. If you find that there are Help topics you refer to over and over, you can mark them with a **bookmark** so that you can locate them quickly. Choose Bookmark and then Define from the Help menu when the topic you want to create the

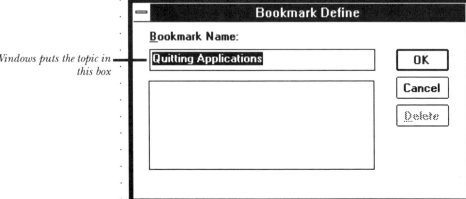

Windows puts the topic in this box

bookmark for is displayed. Then enter a short name for your bookmark and click OK. After you've created a bookmark, you can quickly locate that topic by choosing Bookmark and then clicking on the name you gave it. Windows will take you straight to that topic.

You can also **annotate Help topics** with personal notes about your own problem areas and things you forget all the time. To do this, choose Edit and then Annotate from the Help menu. You'll see a notepad where you can write your notes. After you've annotated a topic, you'll see a paper clip next to its name. Quitting Applications

> *Here's how you can create a custom Help window listing all the keyboard shortcuts you can't remember!*

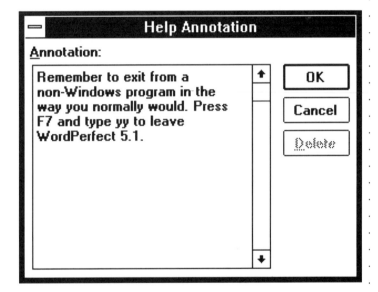

Here's a tip: Instead of annotating a help window or making a bookmark for it, if you want to keep it handy during a session with Windows, just find the topic you need and then minimize the window.

CHAPTER 6

Quick Tips

Here's a rundown of the techniques you saw in this chapter:

Here's How To...	
Change the screen colors	Click on the Control Panel's Color icon; then choose a color scheme or create your own.
Change the desktop pattern	Click on the Desktop icon; then choose Edit Pattern.
Choose a desktop wallpaper	Click on the Desktop icon; then choose a wallpaper.
Change the windows' border width, icon spacing, grid, and/or cursor blink rate	Click on the Desktop icon and choose any of these.
Change the rate keys repeat	Click on the Keyboard icon and change the key repeat rate.
Change the way the mouse operates	Click on the Mouse icon and set the tracking speed, left/right-handed mouse, etc.
Change the system date and time	Click on the Date and Time icon.
Change the date and time format	Click on the International icon.
Create a Help bookmark	Go to the topic and choose Bookmark from the Help menu.
Annotate a Help topic with your own notes	Go to the topic and choose Annotate; then type the notes.

7

PRINTING

You probably installed a printer when you installed Windows, or maybe someone else set it up for you. If you've been printing just fine with no problems, you may not even be interested in this chapter. But if you haven't installed a printer, if you've bought new fonts for your printer, or if you're having trouble printing, you may find some valuable information here.

Windows uses a special utility called the **Print Manager** to do printing. It automatically takes over when you print and sends your print jobs to your printer so that you can keep right on working. If you send a big document to be printed, though, you may have to wait just a bit for it to get to the Print Manager.

The Print Manager

The Print Manager only prints documents created by Windows programs. If you're using a non-Windows program with Windows, print your documents just the way you normally would in the program.

You'll see the **Print Manager icon** at the bottom of the screen while it's printing your documents, if the desktop's not covered with windows.

Print Manager

To check on what the Print Manager is up to, click on its icon. (It's in the Main group if the Print Manager isn't printing.) You can also press Ctrl-Esc to bring up the Task List and then select Print Manager. You'll see the **Print Manager window**. It shows you the status of all your print jobs and lets you change the order they'll be printed in, among other things.

The Print Manager Window

Chapter 7

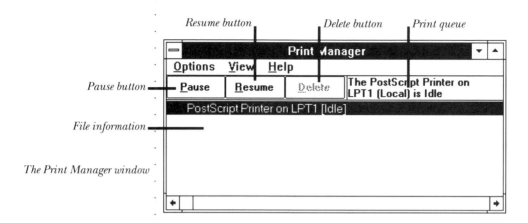

The Print Manager window

Changing the Print Queue
As you send each print job, Print Manager places it in a **queue**, or lineup, and prints each one in the order it gets them, like a short-order cook. You can look at how the documents are lined up in this print queue and change the order they'll be printed in, if you're in a rush for a particular document.

To change the printing order, just drag the icon of the document to a new location in the print queue. You can't change the order of the one that's printing, though (it has a little printer icon to the left of it).

Pausing and Resuming Printing
As you print, you may need to stop the printer temporarily ("pause" it) to stop a paper jam or whatever. To do this, click on the **Pause button**. When you've fixed the problem, click the **Resume button**.

Stop That Job!
If you want to cancel printing of a document that's being printed *right now*, click the **Delete button**. You'll be asked to confirm that you really want to stop printing, so click Cancel in the dialog box. The printer may not stop right away because it will continue to print whatever part of the document has already been sent to it. If you can't live with that, there's always a power switch on your printer.

If you decide that you'd rather not print a document that's waiting in the queue, select it by clicking on it; then click Delete.

If you want to cancel printing *everything*, here's the quick way: just exit the Print Manager (choose Exit from the Options menu or double-click on the Control icon). You'll be asked if that's really what you want to do.

To close the Print Manager window without canceling all your printing, minimize it by clicking on the Minimize icon in the upper-right corner.

You can use the Print Manager's **Options menu** to speed up the printing process. Normally Windows divides the time it pays attention to your programs and to printing about equally. You can choose High Priority to allocate more attention to printing (and thus speed it up and perhaps slow down your work in a program) or Low Priority if the work you're doing is more important than how fast your documents get printed.

Print Speed

The Print Manager sometimes needs to get your attention to deal with printing problems. Your printer may have run out of paper, or paper may have jammed inside it, for example. Normally it will beep once at you and then flash the Print Manager's icon (or the Print Manager's title bar, if you've got it open as a window). You can change the way the Print Manager gets your attention to either have it beep and show you a message box whenever it needs your care, no matter what program you're running, or have the Print Manager ignore the condition and just stop printing whenever it has to. Use the Options menu to change how you want this to work.

Print Manager Messages

If you're sharing printers with other users on a network, printing is just a little different. Normally Windows prints directly to the network without using Print Manager, because it's faster that way. You don't have to change anything. (Of course, you have to remember to log on and select your printer first.)

Network Printing

You can use the Print Manager for network printing if you want to. In some cases it may even be faster than printing directly to the network. Because there are so many different kinds of networks, different printers, and different numbers of users on a network, all I can say is: Try it both ways and see which works best on your network. To print via File Manager over a Network, choose **Network** from the Options menu. Then click on the Print Net Jobs Direct check box to deselect it, if it's selected.

Viewing the Network Queue
You can choose Selected Net Queue from the View menu to see what everybody on the network has in line to be printed on that printer. This can help you decide if you have time to go to lunch before your print job's done. You can even choose View Other Net Queue to see what's in line for another printer on the net, if you want to hunt around for a printer with a shorter queue.

When you do network printing, you don't see the Print Manager's icon, so don't even bother looking for it. If you need to see the Print Manager's window, select the Print Manager from the Main group.

Printing from Non-Windows Programs
If you're printing a document from a non-Windows program, you don't use the Print Manager at all. You just print as you normally would from that program. (Sometimes—a very few sometimes—your document won't print until you exit from Windows.)

You may run into trouble if you try to print some documents from a non-Windows program and then go over to Windows and print with the Print Manager. Windows may get confused with all this happening at the same time. Print non-Windows documents and then print from Windows, or vice versa. It doesn't matter which you do first; just don't do both together and you shouldn't have any problems.

As a last resort, if you're having trouble printing a non-Windows document, you can probably convert it into a format that a Windows program can use. For example, most word processing programs let you convert their documents to ASCII format (sometimes called DOS Text format) or to some "generic word processor" format. The

Notepad and Windows Write can accept and print these files. Microsoft Excel, if you have it, can read dBASE and Lotus 1-2-3 files, as well as other spreadsheet formats.

Adding Printers

You probably installed a printer when you installed Windows, or someone else did. But if you buy a new printer, you may need to know how to install it. This section will tell you how in general, but there's a lot of online help available as you install a particular printer. As you're installing, as soon as you select your printer, choose Help to get specific help about that model of printer.

Adding a Printer

To install a new printer, first find the Windows Setup disks. You're going to need one of them. Then double-click the Control Panel's **Printer** icon. You'll see the Printers dialog box, and it should list any printers that have already been installed. (You can install more than one, and they don't all have to be connected to your computer. If you have one kind of printer at home and another one at work, you can install both of them so that you can format documents for your work printer even if you're working at home. On second thought, maybe you'd rather not do this.)

Printers

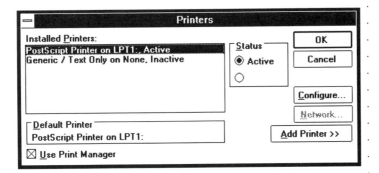

Click on Add Printer; then select your printer from the list that appears. To go quickly to the name of your printer, type the first letter of its name (very handy if yours is a Wang). You can then use the down arrow to

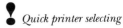 *Quick printer selecting*

Chapter 7

move to the each printer name you want. When your printer is highlighted, click Install. You'll be asked to insert a Windows Setup disk (the screen will tell you which one) so that Windows can copy the information it needs.

If your printer isn't listed, there are two easy things you can do. First, you can get out your printer manual and see if it will emulate another printer that is on the list. Second, you can choose Generic/Text Only. With it, you can print your documents with text but no graphics, at least until you get a call in to Microsoft about what to do about installing your printer. The phone number for Windows technical support is (206) 637-7098. They're constantly adding support for more printers.

You can also choose Unlisted Printer, but you'll need to know where your printer driver files are (and *what* they are), because you'll be asked to tell Windows that.

Configuring a Printer

After you choose which printer you want to install, click Configure. The Printers - Configure dialog box will appear and ask you to assign the printer to a port. In the computer world, there are **parallel ports** and **serial ports**. LPT ports are for parallel printers, and COM ports are for serial printers and things like modems. Chances are yours is a parallel printer, and chances are it's on LPT1. If you don't know what kind of printer you have or which port it's connected to, try those settings and see if they work. (At the end of this chapter, you'll find a way to figure out which port the printer's on, if it's not on LPT1.)

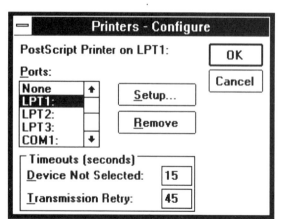

Just leave the Timeouts box alone. The default settings are usually just fine. These settings determine how long Windows waits before it starts giving you messages that something's wrong. If you start getting error messages as you print, you can go back and adjust the default settings later.

Then click **Setup**. You'll see a Setup box specifically for the printer you're installing. What you can choose depends on the printer (this box is for a LaserWriter). Here are a few other things you may be able to choose:

```
┌─────────────────────────────────────────────────┐
│              PostScript Printer on LPT1:        │
├─────────────────────────────────────────────────┤
│  Printer:     [Apple LaserWriter Plus    ▼]    │
│                                          ┌────────┐
│  Paper Source: [Upper Tray         ▼]   │   OK   │
│                                          └────────┘
│  Paper Size:   [Letter 8 ½ x 11 in  ▼]  ┌────────┐
│                                          │ Cancel │
│  ┌─Orientation──┐  ┌─Scaling──────┐     └────────┘
│  │   ● Portrait │  │ [100] percent│     ┌────────┐
│  │ A            │  │              │     │Options…│
│  │   ○ Landscape│  │              │     └────────┘
│  └──────────────┘  │ Copies:  [1] │     ┌────────────┐
│                    └──────────────┘     │Add Printer…│
│                                         └────────────┘
│                                         ┌────────┐
│                                         │ Help…  │
│                                         └────────┘
│                                         ┌────────┐
│                                         │ About… │
│                                         └────────┘
└─────────────────────────────────────────────────┘
```

- **Tractor** is for sheet-fed paper, **Tray** or **Bin** for single-sheet paper.

- Choose **Paper width** and **Paper height** according to the size of the paper you'll be using. The settings for 8.5 in. Letter and 11 in. Letter are standard. The A4 size is slightly narrower and longer, popular in Europe, and B5, wider and shorter, is popular in Japan. Don't choose those last two sizes unless you're using that size paper!

- **Orientation** means the way the text (or graphics) is printed on the page. **Portrait** is standard; **Landscape** is sideways.

- **Cartridges** is a choice if your printer uses font cartridges. You'll see a list box where you can select the ones your printer has.

- **Options...** means that there's another dialog box where you can choose even more options. Click on it to see what those are.

In most cases, Windows' preset settings will be just fine. If you see something you don't understand, you can choose Help for information that is about this printer.

The Active Printer

After you've got everything as you want it, click OK. You'll return to the Printers dialog box, where you can choose which printer you want to be active. You can have more than one active printer, one for each printer port. If you've installed more than one printer, you'll need to tell Windows which one is the **default printer**—the one you want to print with. Windows prints only with the default printer, and it has to be active.

Windows prints with the active default printer.

Look in the Default Printer box to see which printer Windows is going to use as your default printer. If the printer listed there isn't the one you want to print with, double-click on the name of the printer you do want to print with. All of your installed printers are listed right there on the screen.

Network Printers

If you're going to print on a **network printer**, you don't follow the procedure above. Instead, the Network... box in the Printers dialog box will be available (if you're not on a network, it will be gray). Click on that box; then specify your port, the name of the network printer, and your password, and click Connect. The choices you have will depend on the network you're using.

Fonts

If you're new to Windows, you may be surprised to find out that you can now change fonts on the screen! Windows comes with several different fonts that are automatically installed in your system, depending on what kind of printer you have and what kind of display monitor you're using. If you don't believe me, go into Windows Write and use the Character menu to change fonts.

Font Basics

A **font** is basically a collection of characters in a particular typeface. All printers, even laser printers, have at least one font built into them, and it's usually Courier, which looks like this:

```
Courier
```

Yes, it's supposed to look like a typewriter, but why anyone would want to have a several-thousand-dollar laser printer produce "typewriter" type is beyond me. Courier is a **monospaced font**, which means that each letter takes up the same amount of space as any other letter. With a **proportionally spaced font**, like the ones used on this book, each letter takes up a different amount or space; for example, an *i* takes up less space than an *m*. Looks better, yes?

There are basically two different types of fonts: **serif fonts**, which have little things at the ends of the letters, like the text of this book, and **sans serif** fonts, which have very clean lines and are like the text used for the headings in this book. Purists say that serif fonts are easier to read if you're reading a lot at one stretch. I agree with them.

Courier, Times, and Helvetica are the three fonts you'll see most often. On the screen, they look like what you see here.

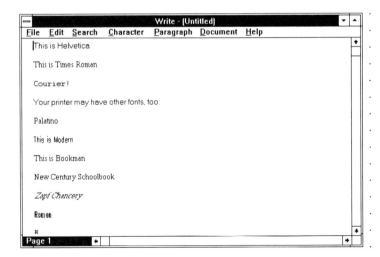

Chapter 7

As you can see, Times is a serif font, Helvetica is sans serif, and Courier... you know what Courier is supposed to be.

Printed, they look like this:

This is Times.

This is Helvetica.

This brings us to another important point: The fonts you see on your screen are called **screen fonts**. (Screen fonts are also sometimes called **raster fonts**.) They *represent* what you get in your documents. Your display monitor often can't display everything just exactly as it will be printed, although line breaks and so on are displayed correctly.

The fonts used to print documents are called **printer fonts**. You'll probably have a wider variety of printer fonts to choose from than screen fonts, but Windows will represent the font that's chosen as closely as it can on the screen.

Fonts are also described in terms of size. A font's size is measured in **points** (1/72 of an inch). Commonly used sizes in printed documents are 10- or 12-point type for text (roughly corresponding to Pica or Elite on a typewriter) and larger point sizes, such as 14 points, for headings. Dot-matrix printers also use the notation cpi (characters per inch) for fonts.

Adding New Fonts

Fonts

You can add new fonts to most laser printers. Usually, when you buy a new font on disk, it comes with both screen and printer versions so that you can see a close approximation on the screen of what you're going to get in your document. It also usually comes with an installation program. If there's an installation program with your new font, use it. It will normally install both the screen fonts and the printer fonts. If an installation program isn't provided, you can install the screen fonts via the Fonts icon on the Control Panel and the printer fonts by using the Printers - Configure dialog box.

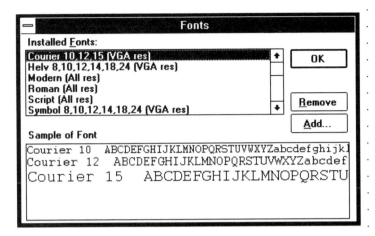

To add new screen fonts, double-click on the Fonts icon. You'll see the Fonts dialog box, listing all the fonts that are installed for your printer. You may not have installed any of these, but they were put there automatically when you installed the printer.

A sample of what the characters in the font look like is shown at the bottom of the box. You can click on the various fonts to see what they will produce. If you see several different sizes listed for a font, that means that it is available only in those sizes. If only one size is shown, the font is what's called a **vector font**. It can be produced in any size, so only one size is listed.

To add a new font to the list, click on Add. Windows will ask you for the name of the font file. It will automatically search the Windows directory for all files ending in .FON if you just click OK. Remember to include A: if the floppy disk with the new font on it's in drive A (you can just click on the [-a-] that's listed under Directories:).

To install printer fonts, click on the Printers icon in the Control Panel. Then click on the printer you want to install the fonts for, in the list of installed printers, and click on Configure. In the Configure dialog box, click on Setup. If that printer can handle soft fonts or cartridge fonts (many printers can't), you'll see a Fonts button. Click on it to go to the Printer Font Installer.

CHAPTER 7

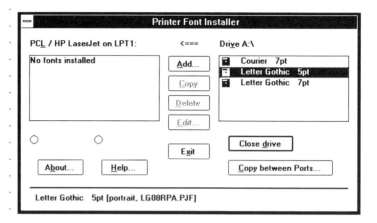

You can then click on Add fonts... or the ever-useful Help button. If you click Add, Windows will ask you to insert the disk with the font files on it in drive A:. If you've already copied the font files onto your hard disk, fill out the dialog box with the name of the drive and directory where the files are. Windows will then search the floppy disk or the directory on your hard disk and display a list of all the font files it finds.

> Once a list of fonts is displayed in the Printer Font Installer, you can click on as many as you like to install them all at once.

> There's a document called PRINTERS.TXT that you can read in the Notepad. It may have some specific information about your particular printer and its capabilities.

> Your printer may have printer fonts that Windows doesn't have screen fonts for. That's OK. Windows will substitute a font on the screen that's about the same size as the printer font.

Removing a Font Fonts use up a lot of memory. If there's one you never use, you can free up some disk space by deleting it. There's a Remove box for screen fonts and a Delete box for printer fonts, depending on which dialog box you're looking at.

Don't delete the Helvetica (or Helv) screen font, though; Windows uses it in dialog boxes!

Managing Fonts

There are a several print utility programs you can purchase that will simplify managing your fonts and let you print a wide variety of fonts in many different sizes (and see them on the screen, too). Zenographics has SuperPrint; their number is (714) 851-6352. Adobe Systems, Inc., has Adobe Type Manager (Windows version); call (415) 961-4400 for details. Both of these programs will let you print PostScript fonts on H-P LaserJets. Bitstream, Inc., has a print utility program called FaceLift that works with Bitstream fonts; you can reach them at (800) 522-3668.

Changing Fonts

Once you've installed a font, you can change to that font within a program like Windows Write or Word for Windows by using the Character menu. You can make text bold, italics, underlined, or superscript or subscript, for example. (Changes like these are called changing the **type style**.) You can also change the point size and make the characters larger or smaller both on the screen and in your printed documents.

Here's the Font menu for Windows Write (choose

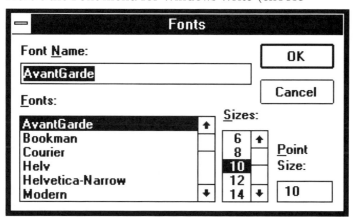

Chapter 7

Character and then Fonts...). (The printer here is an Apple LaserWriter, which has quite a few fonts.)

There are lots of keyboard shortcuts that you can use to change type styles. For example, Ctrl-B switches to bold and Ctrl-I switches to italics. If you use a word processing program a lot with Windows, you'll soon get used to these shortcuts so that you don't have to take your hands off the keyboard.

Troubleshooting Printing Problems

Sometimes things don't always work as you'd like them to, and printing documents is one area where this seems to happen more frequently than most of us would like. If the printer won't print, here are a few things to check for, more or less in order of difficulty.

Check to see that it's on. Check that it has paper. See if the cables are tightly connected.

In Windows, go to the Print Manager and check the printer queue. Try deleting all the print jobs except the top one. If that doesn't do it, check to see that the printer's installed. Check to see that it's the default printer, and that it's active.

If all those things are OK, check to see that your port setting is right. To do this, go out to DOS by clicking on the DOS Prompt icon. Type this:

COPY CON LPT1

TESTING

Then press F6 and Enter.

Wait a minute and see if this prints. If it does, your printer is on LPT1. If not, try LPT2, LPT3, COM1, COM2, and COM3, until you've figured out which port the pesky thing is attached to. Then go back into the Printer dialog box and change the port setting. (Return to Windows by typing exit at the DOS prompt.)

If your printer is a serial printer (if it's on one of the COM ports), go to the Control Panel and double-click on the Ports icon. Then click on the port the printer is on and click on Settings. Check to see that the settings match those for your printer. You may have to get the printer's manual out.

If you've tried all these things and it still won't print, exit Windows and try printing from another program. If it prints from there, you know the problem is somewhere in Windows. Go back into Windows and double-check your setup, including the Printer Setup dialog box in whatever program you're trying to print from (it'll be on the Print menu). If all else fails, install your printer again. Then call Microsoft.

Sometimes the problem is that you're not getting the fonts you asked for. If this happens, it's probably one of two things: either the fonts aren't there (you forgot to download them, or you may have turned the printer off, or there may have been a power failure) or your printer's out of memory. Fonts are memory hogs, and if you're printing graphics, too, you can easily run out of printer memory. To get around this, print the document using the printer's built-in fonts or use fewer fonts in the document. Split the document into smaller files, if it's lots of graphics that's causing the problem.

Here's a rundown of the techniques you saw in this chapter:

Quick Tips

Here's How To...

Print a document	Choose Print from the File menu to use the Print Manager.
Print a non-Windows document	Use the print command in the program.
Check on the Print Manager	Click on its icon, or press Ctrl-Esc and choose it from the Task List

Chapter 7

Here's How To...*(continued)*

Change a document's position in the print queue	Drag the document's icon or use Ctrl-Up or -Down arrow in the Print Manager screen..
Pause the printer	Click Pause or press Alt-P.
Resume printing	Click Resume or press Alt-R.
Stop printing a job or remove a job from the queue	Click Delete or press Alt-D.
Cancel printing everything	Double-click on the Print Manager's Control icon or choose Exit from the Options menu.
Close the Program Manager without cancelling printing	Click on its Minimize icon.
Change print speed, message method, or print on a network	Use the Options menu.
Add a new printer	Click on the Control Panel's Printers icon.
Add new screen fonts	Click on the Control Panel's Fonts icon.
Add new printer fonts	Click on the Control Panel's Printers icon.

8

OH, NO! (TROUBLESHOOTING)

I'm Out of Memory!

Close a few programs. Minimize as many icons as you can. Don't use wallpaper. Empty the Clipboard. Get out of all non-Windows programs. That should do it.

It's Running so S-l-o-w...

If this only happens from time to time, you're probably low on memory. Close a few programs. There are other, more major things you can do to optimize memory, but this is the easiest. The others involve changing various software settings, working with your hardware, or both. If it runs slow all the time, you probably need one of these harder solutions.

Help! I Can't Get Out of My Program!

First, try pressing Esc. Then press Alt-Tab and see if you don't get back to Windows. If not, try pressing Ctrl-C or Ctrl-Break. If this doesn't work, try clicking End Task in the Task List. If you've tried to quit every which way you can, try pressing Ctrl-Alt-Del. This will restart your computer, and you'll lose any work you haven't saved. There's always the On/Off switch, too.

What Are These Different "Modes"?

Windows runs in either Real, Standard, or Enhanced mode, depending on the kind of computer you have. If you have an 80286 computer with at least 1 Mb of memory, Windows will run in Standard mode. If you have an 80386 computer with at least 1 Mb of memory (preferably 2 Mb), Windows will run in Enhanced mode. If you have an older computer like an IBM XT, or if you have less than 1 Mb of memory, Windows runs in Real mode. What's the difference? In Real mode, you are limited by a relatively small memory space, which basically means you can only run one program at a time. In Standard mode, you can run several Windows programs, and you can run non-Windows programs full screen. In Enhanced mode, you can run several Windows and non-Windows programs, all in windows.

It Just Beeps at Me!

Check the title bar. If it says "Select" or "Mark," press the right mouse button, or press Esc. What's happening is that Windows thinks you want to select something to put on the Clipboard.

I Can't Paste into my Non-Windows Program!

You're probably trying to paste graphics, and you won't be able to. There's nothing wrong with you or your program. It just won't work. You can only paste text into most non-Windows programs.

If you're not trying to paste graphics, try this. Assuming what you want to paste is on the Clipboard and the non-Windows program you want to paste it into will only run full screen, start the program and put the cursor where you want the pasted material to go. Then press Alt-Esc to go back to the Program Manager. Click on the program's icon at the bottom of the screen (just click once instead of double-clicking, or you'll open the Control menu); then choose Paste.

If your non-Windows program will run in a window, it's easier. Start the program that you want to paste the Clipboard's contents in and put the cursor where you want the pasted material to go. Then just open the Control menu and choose Paste from the Edit menu.

How the *&*% Do I Select Things to Copy to the Clipboard in a Non-Windows Program?

If you've got a mouse and can run the program in a window, you shouldn't have any problem. Just select with the mouse and use the Control menu's Edit menu to copy. The Windows mouse will take over whenever a program's in a window, so your program doesn't even have to support a mouse.

If you've got a mouse but can only run the program full-screen, you shouldn't have any problem, either, as long as the program you're using can use a mouse. You just use the mouse to select things, but it's a little more complicated to paste them (see the preceding tip).

If the program will run in a window and you *don't* have a mouse, it's even more complicated. Press Alt-Space bar to open the window's Control menu; then choose Edit and Mark. You can then use the keyboard to select text to be copied to the Clipboard. Put the cursor at the start of what you want to copy, press the Shift key, and then press the arrow keys until what you want to copy is highlighted. Press Alt-Space bar again and choose Copy.

If your program can't run in a window and you don't have a mouse, you're out of luck.

When I Press a Key, Something Else Happens!

If you were working in a non-Windows program when this happened, you probably pressed a windows shortcut key combination. If you were in Windows, the key combination you pressed was probably taken over by a non-Windows program you're running. Check the program's PIF file (see below) to see if it reserves any keys for its own use. Uncheck any key combinations that are causing you problems.

I Tiled the Windows, But I Still Can't See Everything!

The Program Manager's probably in the way. Minimize it.

I Can't Quit Windows!

You probably have a non-Windows application running. Go back to it and exit from it normally; then quit Windows. Be sure to save your work if you don't want to lose it!

Help! When I Copy Spreadsheet Data, It's All Jumbled Up!

You're probably using a nonproportional font. In this kind of font, each letter or number takes up a different amount of space. Use a nonproportional font like Courier, or put tabs between the columns.

Oh, No! (Troubleshooting)

Uh, oh. What's a Compatibility Warning?

If you try to run a program that was designed for an earlier version of Windows, you may get a dialog box warning you that you could encounter compatibility problems and suggesting that you update your program. It's best to get an update, but there's one safe way you can run the program until you do. Try running it in Real mode, which makes Windows compatible with older Windows programs, by starting Windows with *win/r* instead of just *win*. You can only run one program at a time in Real mode, though, so get an update soon.

I Can't Run My Pop-Up Programs!

Some "pop-up" or terminate and stay-resident (TSR) programs, like SuperKey and SideKick, need to be started *after* you start Windows. Add the program to a group in the Program Manager (see Chapter 4) and then double-click on it to start it. If it still doesn't work, check the PIF file, if it has one (see below), and see if there's a shortcut key conflict between what you use to start the pop-up program and what Windows wants to use. If it doesn't have a PIF file, you'll need to create one for it (see below).

I Can't Run my Non-Windows Program!

Setup will recognize most programs as either Windows or Non-Windows applications, but for some programs, you may have to use the PIF editor to set up a Program Information File. To do this, click on the PIF editor icon (it's in the Accessories group) and fill out the information it needs. You may have to refer to the program's manual for any special instructions it needs to load.

After you've created your PIF file, restart Windows so that it can read what you've done. If you have to change the PIF file later, be sure to restart Windows again. Every time you change it, Windows needs to read what you changed.

If you use a non-Windows program a lot, (and if you have a 386 computer), you can create a special key shortcut for the program that will let you switch directly to its active window even if you have a lot of windows open on the desktop. To do this, use the PIF editor. Open the PIF file for the non-Windows program (choose File and then Open). Click on the Advanced button and then ignore everything you see except the line that says Application Shortcut Key. Press either Alt or Ctrl plus the key you want to use as a shortcut. Don't use any of the ones in the Reserve Shortcut Keys' box. Also, don't use any of the others that Windows uses, such as Alt-F for File. Here are a few that haven't been taken: Alt-L, Ctrl-Y, Alt-7.

What Was That Phone Number Again?

(206) 637-7098. Microsoft Technical Support will be glad to hear from you.

A

APPENDIX

Here's How To...

Add a document to a program item	Add the document's name to the end of the command line in the Program Item Properties dialog box. (Choose New from the Program Manager's File menu; then choose New Program Item.)
Add a program to a group via Setup	Double-click on the Setup icon (Main group); choose Options and then Set Up Applications. Pick which drive or directory to search; click on the program you want to add, and then click OK.
Add a program to a Program Manager group	Open both a File Manager window and a group window. Drag the program's icon from the File Manager to the group.
Add an item to a group	Copy or move the program's icon into the group (press Ctrl and drag to copy it; drag to move it). Or choose New from the Program Manager's File menu; click Program Item; fill out a description and a command line.
Add a new printer	Click on the Control Panel's Printer icon.
Add new fonts	Click on the Control Panel's Fonts icon.
Annotate a Help topic with your own notes	Go to the topic and choose Annotate; then type the notes.
Associate documents with a program	Select the document and choose Associate from the File Manager's File menu; enter the command used to run the program.

Here's How To...*(continued)*

Cancel a print job	Highlight the job and click Delete in the Print Manager window, or press Alt-D.
Cancel printing everything	Double-click on the Print Manager's Control icon or choose Exit from the Options menu.
Cascade windows	Choose Cascade from the Windows menu, or press Shift-F5.
Change the file information display	Use the View menu.
Change how File Manager windows appear	Use the Options menu.
Change an item's icon	Choose Change Icon and View Next in the Program Item Properties dialog box.
Change the system date and time	Click on the Control Panel's Date and Time icon.
Change print speed, message method, or print on a network	Use the Print Manager's Options menu.
Change a group's name	Click its icon; choose File and then Properties.
Change the current drive	Click on a drive icon in the Directory Tree window
Change the rate keys repeat	Click on the Keyboard icon and change the key repeat rate (Control Panel).
Change the screen colors	Click on the Control Panel's Color icon; then choose a color scheme or create your own.
Change the way the mouse operates	Click on the Mouse icon and set the tracking speed, left/right handed mouse, etc.
Change a document's position in the print queue	Drag the document's icon or use Ctrl-Up or -Down arrow in the Print Manager screen.

Here's How To...*(continued)*

Change the windows' border width, icon spacing, grid, and/or cursor blink rate	Click on the Control Panel's Desktop icon and choose any of these.
Change the desktop pattern	Click on the Control Panel's Desktop icon; then choose Edit Pattern.
Choose a desktop wallpaper	Click on the Control Panel's Desktop icon; then choose a wallpaper.
Choose an item in a dialog box	Click on the selection, or type Alt-*letter* (where *letter* is the letter in the box).
Close the Directory Tree window	Choose Exit from the File menu, or double-click on the File Manager's Control icon, or choose End Task for the File Manager from the Task List.
Close a window	Double-click on its Control icon (or press Alt-F4 in application windows; Ctrl-F4 in document windows).
Close a group window	Double-click on its Control icon or press Ctrl-F4.
Close the Program Manager without cancelling printing	Click on its Minimize icon.
Collapse the display	Click on the root directory icon.
Collapse the directory (assuming it's got a + on it)	Press + or click on it.
Copy a program icon to another group	Press Ctrl and drag it.
Copy text	Select; then choose Copy from an Edit menu (or press Ctrl-Ins).
Copy files and directories on the same disk	Select; then Ctrl-drag, or press F8 and use the Copy command.
Copy files and directories onto a different disk	Select; then drag, or press F8 and use the Copy command.

Here's How To...(continued)

Copy floppy disks	Choose Copy Diskette from the File Manager's Disk menu.
Create a Help bookmark	Go to the topic and choose Bookmark from the Help menu.
Create a new group	Choose New from the Program Manager's File menu; click Program Group; fill out a description and a command line.
Create a new directory	Click on the directory you want the new one to appear *under*; then choose Create Directory from the File Manager's File menu.
Cut text	Select; then choose Cut from an Edit menu (or press Shift-Del).
Cycle windows	Press Ctrl-F6 or choose Next from the Control directory windows menu.
Delete a group	Click its icon; choose File and Delete.
Delete a file or directory	Select it; then choose Delete from the File menu.
Deselect all files	Press Ctrl-\.
Exit from the Program Manager	Double-click on its Control icon, or highlight Program Manager and click on End Task in the Task List, or press Alt-F4 when the Program Manager window is active.
Exit from Windows	Exit from the Program Manager.
Expand all the subdirectories of all of the directories	Press Ctrl-Gray * or choose Expand All from the Tree menu.
Expand all the selected directory's subdirectories	Press * or choose Expand Branch from the Tree menu (File Manager).
Expand a selected directory one level (assuming it's got a - on it)	Press -, click on it, or choose Expand One Level from the Tree menu (File Manager).

Here's How To...*(continued)*

Format floppy disks	Choose Format Diskette from the File Manager's Disk menu
Get help	Click on Help on the menu bar, press Alt-H, or, to get the help index, press F1.
Get the help index	Press F1.
Go to DOS	Click on the DOS Prompt icon in the Main group.
Go up one level	Click on [..] in a directory window (press Home to go directly to it).
Maximize a group window	Double-click on its title bar or click on its Maximize icon.
Maximize a window	Click on its Maximize icon or choose Maximize from its Control menu.
Minimize a window	Click on its Minimize icon or choose Minimize from its Control menu.
Move between group windows	Click in the one you want, or press Ctrl-F6 or Ctrl-Tab.
Move to another selection in the same window	Click or use the arrow keys.
Move files and directories	Select; then drag, or press F7 and use the Move on the same disk command.
Move a window	Drag it by its title bar or use the Control menu's Move command.
Move through a window	Drag or click in the scroll bars, or click on the arrow icons.
Move a program icon to another group	Drag it.
Move within a dialog box	Click in it, or press Tab to move forward or Shift-Tab to move backward.
Move files and directories onto a different disk	Select; then Alt-drag, or press F7 and use the Move command.

Here's How To...(*continued*)

Open a document	Choose Open from a File menu (or press Alt-F and type O).
Open a new document	Choose New from a File menu (or press Alt-F and type N).
Open a directory window	Double-click on a directory icon or press Enter when the icon is highlighted.
Open a window	Double-click on its icon or press Enter when the icon is highlighted.
Paste	Select; then choose Paste from an Edit menu (or press Shift-Ins).
Pause the printer	Click Pause in the Print Manager window or press Alt-P.
Print ASCII files on the default printer	Choose Print from the File Manager's File menu.
Print a Windows document	Choose Print from the File menu to use the Windows Print Manager.
Print a non-Windows document	Use the print command in the program
Rename a file or directory	Select it; then choose Rename from the File Manager's File menu.
Replace the contents of each subsequent directory window instead opening new ones	Choose Replace on Open from the File Manager's View menu.
Restore a window to its previous size	Click on its Restore icon or choose Restore from its Control menu.
Resume printing	Click Resume in the Print Manager window or press Alt-R.
Return to Windows from DOS	Type *exit* at the DOS prompt.

Here's How To...(continued)

Run a program from the Program Manager	Double-click on its icon.
Save a document	Choose Save from a File menu (or press Alt-F and type S).
Save a new document	Choose Save As from a File menu (or press Alt-F and type A).
Scroll a list dialog box	Click on the up or down arrow in the scroll box, or type Alt-*letter* and then press the down arrow key.
Search for a file	Select Search from the File Manager's File menu.
Search for a file by date	Select Sort by and Modification Date from the File Manager's View menu.
See what's on the Clipboard	Double-click on the Clipboard icon in the Main group.
Select the first file in a directory window	Press Home.
Select the last file in a directory window	Press End.
Select a file or directory	Click on it, or type the first letter of its name.
Select from menus	Click on the item or press Alt and type the underlined letter or number. When the pull-down menu appears, click on the item, or type the underlined letter or number. You can also highlight the name with the arrow keys and press Enter.
Select all files	Press Ctrl-/.
Select nonadjacent files directories	Alt-click, or press Shift-F8, use the arrow keys, and use the space bar to select.
Select adjacent files and directories	Shift-click, or use Shift and the arrow keys.
Shrink a group window to an icon	Double-click on its Control menu or click on its Minimize icon.

Here's How To...(continued)

Size a window	Drag it outward or inward by its corner, or use the Control menu's Size command.
Start a program	Double-click on its icon, or choose Run from the Program Manager's or File Manager's File menu, or double-click on the DOS Prompt icon and use DOS, or press Enter when the icon is highlighted.
Start a program from the File Manager	Double-click on its icon, or use the Run command, or drag a document icon on top of its program icon, or double-click on an associated document icon.
Start a new document	Choose New from a File menu (or press Alt-F and type N).
Start Windows	Type *win* at the DOS prompt.
Stop printing a job or remove a job from the queue	Click Delete or press Alt-D in the Print Manager.
Switch to a different window	Click in it, or double-click on its name in the Task List, or press Ctrl-Tab for document windows, Alt-Esc for application windows.
Quit Windows	Double-click on the Program Manager's Control icon, or highlight Program Manager and click on End Task in the Task List, or press Alt-F4 when the Program Manager window is active.
Tile directory windows	Press Shift-F4 or choose Tile from the Window menu.
Tile windows	Choose Tile from the Windows menu or press Shift-F4.
Undo what you just did	Choose Undo from an Edit menu (or press Alt-Backspace).
Use wildcards	The * stands for any combination of characters, and ? stands for any one character.

Appendix

Keyboard Shortcuts

To	Use
General	
Get the help index	F1
Open a file	Enter
Bring up the Task List	Ctrl-Esc
Cascade windows	Shift-F5
Tile windows	Shift-F4
Move to another selection in the same window	Arrow keys
Choose highlighted item from a menu	Enter
Cancel a menu	Esc
Move between menus	Arrow keys
Open and close a Control menu	Alt-Space bar; Alt-Hyphen
Switch to the next open program	Alt-Esc
Switch to the next open program, restoring minimized programs	Alt-Tab
Toggle between full-screen and windowed sizes	Alt-Enter
Exit Windows (when Program Manager is active)	Alt-F4

To	Use
In a document	
Copy	Ctrl-Ins
Cut	Shift-Del
Paste	Shift-Ins
Delete	Del
Move to the next or previous line	Down arrow or Up arrow
Move to the next or previous word	Ctrl-Right arrow or Ctrl-Left arrow
Move to the end or beginning of a line	End or Home
Move to the end or beginning of the document	Ctrl-End or Ctrl-Home
Move to the next or previous screen	PgDn or PgUp
Undo what you just did	Alt-Backspace
In a dialog box	
Move between selections	Tab or Shift-Tab
Move to a selection	Alt plus underlined letter
Move to the first or last item	Home or End
Open a drop-down list box	Alt-Down arrow
Select an item in a list box	Space bar
Select a check box	Space bar
Select all items in a list box	Ctrl-/
Select a command button	Enter
Close the box without selecting	Esc or Alt-F4

To	Use
To extend a selection	
To the next or previous line	Shift-Down arrow or Shift-Up arrow
To the end or beginning of the line	Shift-End or Shift-Home
Down or up one window	Shift-End or Shift-Home
Down or up one window	Shift-PgDn or Shift-PgUp
To the next or previous word	Ctrl-Shift-Right arrow or Ctrl-Shift-Left arrow
To the end or beginning of the document	Ctrl-Shift-End or Ctrl-Shift-Home
In the Program Manager	
Get help on the Program Manager	Alt-H
Move between group windows	Ctrl-F6 or Ctrl-Tab
Start a highlighted icon	Enter
Close a group window	Ctrl-F4
Exit from the Program Manager (Windows)	Alt-F4
In the File Manager	
Get help on the File Manager	Alt-H
Open a directory	Enter
Expand a collapsed directory one level	+

To	Use
Expand all the selected directory's subdirectories	*
Expand all the subdirectories of all of the directories	Ctrl-*
Collapse a directory	– (hyphen)
Move a file or directory	F7
Copy a file or directory	F8
Select a file	Type the first letter of its name
Select the first file in the window	Home
Select the last file in the window	End
Select all files in a window	Ctrl-/
Deselect all files	Ctrl-\

INDEX

[..] symbol, 55
286 computer, 1
386 computer, 1, 94
386 Enhanced utility, 84
Accessories group, programs in, 4, 40
active printer, 104
active window, 5, 18
adding documents to groups, 45-46
adding programs to groups, 42-45, 46-48
  with the File Manager, 73-74, 81
Adobe Type Manager, 109
alphabetizing a file display, 70
Alt key shortcuts, 5
Alt-dragging, to move files and directories, 65, 80
Alt-Enter, to switch to full-screen window, 25
Alt-Esc
  to cycle through application windows, 19, 24
  to cycle through programs, 36, 38
Alt-F4, to close a window, 17, 24
annotating Help topics, 95, 96
application windows, 17-18
arranging icons, 23
arranging windows, 21-22, 49
ASCII format, 100

associating programs and documents, 7, 72-73, 81
asterisk, as wildcard, 65
attributes, changing file, 77

Bitstream fonts, 109
bookmark, creating a, 94-95, 96
border, of window, 5
border width, changing, 91, 96
browse, in Help, 12
bus mouse, 2

C:\ prompt, 2
calculator, 4
Calendar, 4, 40
canceling all print jobs, 99, 11
capacities, of floppy disks, 75-76
Cardfile, 40
Cascade command, 21-22, 24
cascading windows, 21-22, 24, 49, 60, 79
changing directories, 30, 45
check boxes, 16
clicking, 3
Clipboard, 1, 39
  tips for using, 33
  uses for, 9
  using the, 31-33, 38
  using with non-Windows programs, 145
Close All Directories command, 61
closing a window, 7, 17

collapsing directories, 57-58, 79
color palette, 85-86
color refiner cursor, 86-87
color schemes
  creating, 85-86
  predefined, 84-85
  saving, 86
Color utility, 83
colors, changing screen, 84-87, 96
colors, hints for, 86
.COM extension, for programs, 28
COM ports, 102
  specifying, 94
  testing, 110
command buttons, 17
Control icon, 7, 17
Control menu, 7
  for copying and pasting, 32
  using to move and resize windows, 20
  using to close group windows, 41
Control Panel, 39
  uses for, 9
  utilities in, 83-84
converting text formats, 100-101
Copy command, 31, 38, 64-65, 80
Copy Diskette command, 74-75, 81
copying files, 63-65, 80
copying floppy disks, 74-75, 81

131

Index

copying icons, 23, 43
copying programs, 50
copying text and graphics, 31-32, 38, 114-115
copying the screen's contents, 32, 38
correcting mistakes, 34-35
creating directories, 66, 80
Ctrl-clicking, 62, 63, 67, 80
Ctrl-dragging, to copy files and directories, 65, 80
Ctrl-F4, to close a window, 17, 24
Ctrl-Ins, as Copy shortcut, 31-32
Ctrl-Tab, to cycle through document windows, 19, 24, 60
currency, changing, 93
current drive, changing the, 56, 79
cursor, blink rate of, 91, 96
custom colors, creating, 86-87
customizing the mouse, 92-93, 96
Cut command, 31, 38
cutting text and graphics, 31-32, 34, 38

date and time, setting, 93, 96
date and time format, changing, 93-94, 96
date, locating files by, 69
Date/time utility, 84
default printer, the, 104
definitions, getting in Help, 13
deleting a group, 48
deleting files and directories, 67, 80
deleting text and graphics, 34-35, 38
deselecting, 62, 80
desktop, 2
  moving icons to the, 23
desktop patterns, changing, 87-89, 96
Desktop utility, 84

dialog boxes, 5, 6
  moving, 20
  using, 15-16, 24
directories, 54-55
  changing, 30, 45
  copying, 63-64, 80
  creating, 66, 80
  deleting, 67-68, 80
  expanding and collapsing, 57-58
  moving through, 58-59, 79
  moving, 66, 80
  renaming, 66, 80
  seeing contents of, 29
  selecting, 62
directory icons, 27-28
directory windows, 58
  locating minimized, 60-61
  managing, 60-62
Directory Tree window, 55-58
  closing, 61
  using to create a new directory, 66
disk drives, represented in File Manager, 56
disks, copying and formatting, 74-77, 81
display, sorting a file, 70, 81
document, adding to a group, 50
document files, 51
document icons, 28
document
  opening an existing, 29, 38
  starting a new, 29, 37
documents
  adding to groups, 45-46
  associating with programs, 72-73, 81
document windows, 17-19
DOS commands, starting programs with, 28-29, 37
DOS prompt, 2, 9, 26, 37, 39
DOS Prompt icon, 28-29, 37
DOS Text format, 100

double arrowhead, as pointer shape, 20
double-clicking, 4
  defining the rate of, 92, 96
  on desktop icon vs. icon in window, 36
double-density disks, 75-76
dragging, 4
  to start a program, 71-72, 81
  to move or copy files and directories, 65, 80

Edit menu, on Control menu, 33
Edit menu, 31, 38
elite type, 107
ellipsis, to indicate dialog box, 6, 15
Enhanced mode, 94, 114
Enter, using to select in dialog boxes, 17
erasing files and directories. See deleting files and directories
Esc, to get out of dialog box, 15
.EXE extension, for programs, 28
exiting from Windows, 7, 8, 37, 38, 49
expanding directories, 57-58, 79
extensions
  for programs, 28
  for different types of files, 51-53
  for associating documents, 72

F1, to get Help, 11
FaceLift, 109
file display, sorting, 70
File Manager, 39
  adding programs to groups with the, 73-74, 81
  closing, 61
  functions of, 9

INDEX

keyboard shortcuts in, 78
locating the, 58
minimizing the, 61
printing from the, 77, 81
purposes of, 51
saving settings of, 62
starting programs with the, 27-28, 71-73, 81
File Manager display, changing the, 77, 81
File menu, 29, 37-38
files, alphabetizing, 70
files
   copying and moving, 63-65, 80
   deleting, 67, 80
   finding, 68-71
   naming, 52-54
   organizing, 54-55
   protecting, 77, 81
   renaming, 66, 80
   selecting, 62-63, 80
   types of, 51-52
   viewing details of, 69-70, 81
finding hidden windows, 22
finding the Program Manager, 26
floppy disks
   capacities of, 75
   copying, 74-75, 81
   formatting, 76-77, 81
   font sizes, 107
fonts
   adding new, 106-107, 111
   removing, 108
   using, 104-110
Fonts utility, 83
formatting floppy disks, 76-77, 81
full-screen size, 1
full-screen windows, 21, 25

Games, 8, 10, 40
granularity, changing, 91
graphics, cutting and copying, 32
grid, for desktop, 91

group
   changing name of a, 48
   creating a new, 49
   deleting a, 48
group icons, 7, 40
   moving, 41
group windows, 40
   manipulating, 49
groups
   creating your own, 7, 42-45
   deleting, 50
   in Program Manager, 8
   groups of files, selecting, 62, 80
Help, getting, 10, 11-13, 23, 49
   customizing, 94-95
Help index, 11
hidden windows, finding, 22
high-density disks, 75-76
hue, 87

I-beam, as insertion point, 16
IBM AT, 1
icons
   arranging, 23
   assigning, 45
   changing, 45, 50
   changing description of, 73
   changing spacing between, 90-91
   copying, 23
   defined, 2
   deleting, 43, 48
   desktop, 3
   for documents, directories, and programs, 28
   group, 7, 40
   in File Manager, 59
   moving, 41, 43, 50
   moving to desktop, 23
   names of, 43
   of Main group, 8-9
Include command, 71
insertion point, 16, 34

installing a printer, 101-104, 111
interface, the Windows, 1
international options, changing, 93-94
International utility, 84
invisible grid for desktop, 91

key repeat rate, changing, 91-92, 96
keyboard shortcuts, 128
   in Program Manager, 49
   in File Manager, 78
keyboard, using for shortcuts, 14
Keyboard utility, 84

laser printers, and COM port, 94
left-handed mouse, 92-93
list boxes, 16
lists, moving to items in, 30
locking a file, 77, 81
LPT ports, 102
luminosity, 86-87

Macintosh, Windows and, 1
Main group, 8, 39
   icons of, 8-9
making a window active, 18
Maximize icon, 5, 6-7, 20, 24
maximizing group windows, 49
maximizing windows, 20-21, 24
measurements, units of, changing, 94
memory, when using wallpaper, 90
menu bar, 5
   in application windows, 18
menu shortcuts, 15
menus, 5
   keyboard shortcuts on, 14
   selecting from, 14-15, 23

133

Index

messages, from Print Manager, 99, 111
Minimize icon, 5, 6-7, 20, 24
Minimize on Use command, 40
minimizing directory windows, 60, 61, 79
minimizing Directory Tree windows, 61, 79
minimizing windows, 20-21, 23, 24, 60, 61, 79
modems, and COM port, 94
modes, running Windows in different, 114
monospaced fonts, 105
mouse, 3-4
   customizing the, 92-93, 96
   mouse, need for, 2
   pointer of, 3
   left-handed, 92-93
   using with non-Windows programs, 115
Mouse utility, 83
Move command, 20, 65
moving dialog boxes, 20
moving directories, 66, 80
moving files, 63, 65, 80
moving icons, 23
moving in documents, 34
moving in windows, 49
moving program icons, 43, 50
moving through windows and documents, 13, 23
moving windows, 19-20, 24

naming files, 52-64
network printing, 99-100, 104
Network utility, 84
New command, 29, 37
New Program Object dialog box, 42-43
non-Windows program icon, on desktop, 46
non-Windows programs, 1
   adding to groups, 46-48
   copying and pasting between, 32-33

   creating key shortcuts for, 117
   cutting and pasting into, 114-115
   printing from, 100
Non-Windows applications group, 9
Notepad, 40

Open command, 29, 38
opening a document, 29, 38
option buttons, 16

Paintbrush, 40
   using to create wallpaper, 90
parallel ports, 102
Paste command, 31, 38
pasting text and graphics, 31-33, 38
path, 27, 55
   using when associating documents with programs, 73
PATH command (DOS), 27
patterns, changing desktop, 87-89, 96
pausing the printer, 98, 111
PgUp, PgDn keys, to scroll dialog boxes, 16
pica type, 107
PIF Editor, 40
PIF files, 117
pointer, 3
   as double arrowhead, 20
points, as measurements, 106
pop-up programs, 116
Ports utility, 83
print queue, 98
Print Manager, 39
   functions of, 9
   icon for, 97
   locating, 97, 111
   messages in, 99
   minimizing, 99, 111
   Options menu in, 99
   window of, 97-98
Print Screen key, 32, 38
printer fonts, 106, 107-108

printer, installing a, 101-104, 111
Printers utility, 84
PRINTERS.TXT, 108
printing a document, 97-101, 111
printing from the File Manager, 77, 81
printing from non-Windows programs, 100
printing on a network, 99-100, 104
printing order, changing the, 98, 111
printing problems, troubleshooting, 110-111
printing, stopping, pausing, and resuming, 98-99, 111
problems with Windows, fixing, 113-117
program, adding to a group, 49
program files, 51
program icons, 28
   deleting, 50
program, starting, 48
Program Group Properties dialog box, 43, 44-45
Program Manager, 2
   closing, 17
   exiting from, 7, 8, 37, 38, 49
   groups in, 8, 39-40
   locating the, 7-8, 26
   minimizing the, 40
   running in background, 7
   starting programs with the, 26-27, 36, 48
   keyboard shortcuts in, 49, 128
programs
   adding to groups, 43-45
   adding to groups with the File Manager, 73-74, 81
   associating with documents, 72-73, 81

INDEX

starting duplicate copies of, 46
starting with the Program Manager, 26-28, 37, 48
starting with the File Manager, 71-73, 81
switching between, 36, 38
proportionally spaced fonts, 105
protecting a file, 77, 81
pull-down menus, 5, 15

question mark, as wildcard, 65

raster fonts, 106
readme files, printing, 77
Real mode, 114
Recorder, 40
renaming directories, 66, 80
renaming files, 66, 80
Replace on Open command, 60, 79
replacing text in Windows Write, 35
resizing windows, 5, 20, 24
Restore icon, 21
restoring a window's size, 21, 24
restoring deleted text, 34
resuming a print job, 98, 111
returning to Windows from DOS, 28, 48
Reversi, 10
root directory, defined, 54
Run command, 26, 37
Run Minimized command, 27
running programs, 26-28, 37

sans serif fonts, 105
saturation, 87
Save As command, 30, 38
Save Changes command, 22-23

Save command, 30, 38
saving a document, 30, 38
saving color schemes, 86
saving contents of Clipboard, 34
screen colors, changing, 84-87, 96
screen, copying the, 32, 38
screen fonts, 106-107
scroll bars, 5, 6, 13
scrolling, 13
  while selecting, 35
Search command, 68-69
searching, in Help, 12
selecting from menus, 14-15, 23
selecting text, 35-36, 38
selections, extending, 35
"Select" message, 33, 37
serial mouse, 2
serial ports, 102
serial printers, 111
serif fonts, 105
Setup disks, using for installing new printers, 101
Setup program, using, 50
Shift-clicking, 35, 62, 63, 67, 80
  to copy large selections, 32
Shift-Del, as Cut shortcut, 31-32
Shift-F4, to tile windows, 22, 24, 60
Shift-F5, for cascading windows, 22, 24, 60
Shift-Ins, as Paste shortcut, 31-32
Shift-Tab, using in dialog box, 15, 24
Size command, 20
Solitaire, 10
sorting a display, 70
Sound utility, 84
source and destination, 74
spacing between icons, 90-91
special characters, in file names, 52-53

Standard mode, 114
starting a new document, 29, 37
starting programs
  with the Program Manager, 26-28, 37, 48
  with the File Manager, 71-73, 81
starting Windows, 2
status line, in File Manager, 75
subdirectories, 54-55, 57
  creating, 66, 80
subtrees. See subdirectories
SuperPrint, 109
switching between programs, 36, 38

Tab, using in dialog box, 15, 16, 24
Task List, 7-8
  displaying, 19
  using to find hidden windows, 7-8, 22, 26, 97, 111
Terminal, 40
text boxes, 16
text, copying (non-Windows programs), 33-34
text files, printing from the File Manager, 77, 81
Tile command, 21-22, 24
tiling windows, 21-22, 24, 49, 60, 79
title bar, 5
  using to maximize a group window, 41
transferring data, 1
tree structure, of directories, 54
Tree menu, 58
troubleshooting problems, 113-117
TSR programs, 116
type style, changing the, 109
typeface. See font
  functions of, 9
  running, 46-48

135

Index

typematic rate, changing, 91-92
.TXT extension, for Notepad, 30
Undo command, 31, 34, 38
units of measurement, changing, 93

vector fonts, 107
View menu, using, 69-70

wallpaper, using, 89-90, 96
wildcards, using, 65
   using to delete files, 67
   using in searches, 68
   using to restrict displays, 71
window, active, 5
Window menu, 36, 41-42, 60-61
windows
   arranging, 21-22, 49
   borders of, changing, 91, 96
   cascading, 49
   closing group, 40, 49
   closing, 7, 17, 24
   elements of, 5-6
   maximizing, 6-7, 20-21, 24
   minimizing, 6-7, 20-21, 24
   moving, 19-20, 24
   moving in, 49
   moving between, 19, 24
   opening, 24
   resizing, 5, 20, 24
   tiling, 49
   types of, 17-18
Windows applications groups, 9
Windows
   exiting from, 7, 8, 37, 38, 49
   previous versions of, 116
Windows program menus, using, 29-31, 37-38
Windows Setup, 39
Windows Write, 40
.WRI extension, for Windows Write, 30

Colophon

The *Little Windows Book* was written in WordPerfect 5.1 running under Windows on a 386 DOS computer. Screen shots were taken in Tiffany Plus, a program provided through the courtesy of Anderson Consulting and Software of Bonneville, WA. Text and graphics were sent over a TOPS network to a Macintosh II, where page makeup was done in Aldus PageMaker. *Ain't technology grand?*

The design is the Peachpit Press Little Book series design by Robin Williams. Body text is ITC New Baskerville and headings are Futura Bold, both from Adobe Systems, Incorporated.

The publisher and the author have donated a percentage of the book's cost to organizations involved in reforestation and forest protection.